The Golem of Church Street

An Artist's Reflection on the New Anti-Semitism

DAVID SOKOL

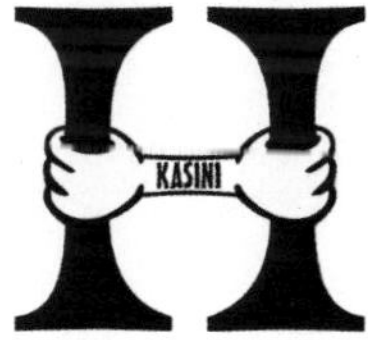

The Golem of Church Street
An Artist's Reflection on the New Anti-Semitism

Kasini House Books
PO Box 1025
Burlington, VT 05402
802-264-4839
www.kasinihouse.com

First printing, Kasini House Books. Printed in Vermont, United States.

Cover Image: *Golem of Church Street* by David Sokol
                 (9"x17", woodblock print, 2008)

ISBN: 0-9771397-3-5
        978-0-9771397-3-6

The book, *The Golem of Church Street* came about when we encouraged David Sokol to create a series of prints about an emerging and new anti-Semitism.

Traditional anti-Jewish prejudice exercised a litany of falsehoods and misrepresentations of Jewish life, belief, and practices to justify the suppression of the Jewish people, essentially regulating them to second-class citizens. Jews were routinely used as the scapegoats for economic and political woes of the larger society. The practice of anti-Semitism included exclusion and acts of violence against property and persons. Since World War II, Western civilization has been engaged in a process of undoing anti-Semitism though education, dialogue, political and legal reform.

What is the new anti-Semitism? Jews are once again emerging as targets of hate and prejudice. This new anti-Semitism is particularly virulent in matters related to Israel, the Middle East, and terrorism. Jews are increasingly seen as the reason the Muslim world is angry with the United States. The blame for the suffering of the Palestinian people is laid at the feet of the Jewish people, whether they live in Israel or not. Jews are equated with Israel, with the Nazis. They are portrayed as indirectly responsible for terrorism. This new anti-Semitism is not expressed as graffiti on the synagogue door. It laces the rhetoric of news reporting and political action. It is spoken at rallies, in emphatic speeches political neophytes. It is present in political art about Israel and Palestine. It can be found in blogs and YouTube videos.

Adding insult to injury, perpetrators of this new anti-Semitism are often former allies of the Jewish people, particularly those of the political Left who championed the Jewish people for much of the 20th century.

The Golem of Church Street is a piece of a larger cultural dialogue. It is not intended to be comprehensive. It is simply one artist's reaction to the anti-Semitism of our times. The prints presented here are a reaction to the new anti-Semitism. The accompanying texts are artist statements meant to inform the viewer's understanding of the artist's thinking. Statements presented as fact have been vetted and sourced at the end of the book.

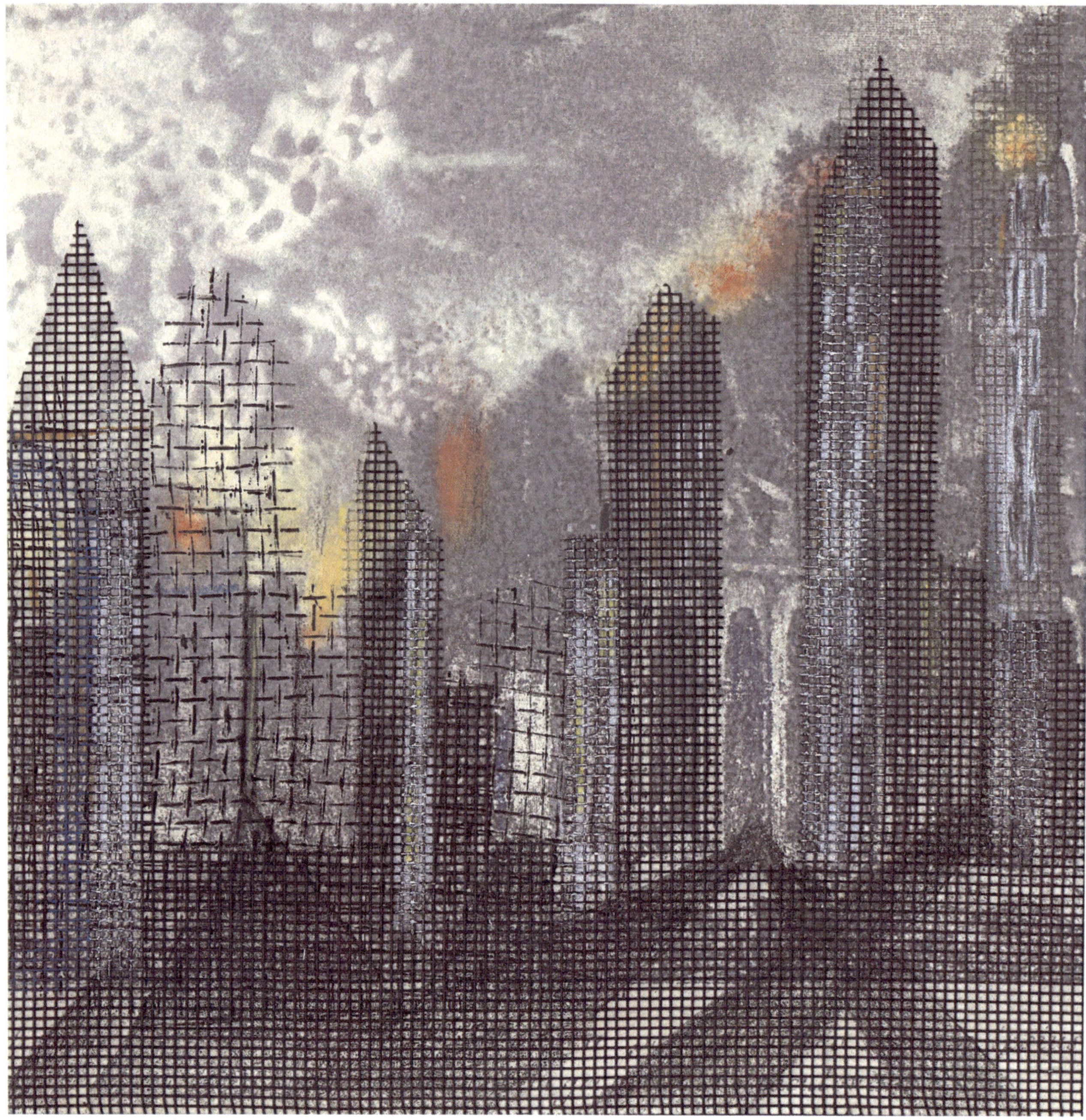

Introduction

Imagine life in America!

 People all over the world imagine that citizens of the United States live in a town dotted by clapboard houses with white picket fences; a town with a village square and a church at the head of the main street. Kids walk safely to school. Town meetings end with a lighthearted bantering of views. Few Americans live in this picture postcard, but it does exist. Vermont is full of towns that mirror this idealistic setting.

Vermont is full of entrepreneurs. They make ice cream and roast high-quality coffee for distribution throughout the country. Vermont manufactures teddy bears to hug and weed whackers on wheels for old people to take care of their lawns. Vermont has as many psychotherapists per capita as San Francisco and one of the best teaching hospitals in the country. The state has two senators and a congressman who are not in the pockets of special interests; who vote what they think is good. Vermont prides itself on being tolerant of others and a welcoming place.

Yet, even in Vermont anti-Semitism creeps like mold into the rants of the self-righteous. In this idyllic America, misguided and self-appointed champions blame the "Jews" for the suffering of Palestinians. Lecturers advocate the end of the Jewish state. Academics and political wanna-bes propose we abandon financial aid to Israel and let them "stand on their own." These people hold Israel to a double standard. They claim American Jews control Congress; that Jews were involved in a conspiracy to blow up the World Trade Center. Artists compare Israelis to Nazis. Political groups demonize Israel and glorify terrorists.

These acts and attitudes fit the State Department's definition of anti-Semitism found in their 2004 Report on Global Anti-Semitism.

etching and collage
on paper printed
at sokolpress

Unfortunately, such prejudice makes Vermont reflective of a dangerous segment of America—a small segment, but one that is growing beyond the fringe.

John Mearsheimer at the University of Chicago and Stephen Walt at Harvard's Kennedy School of Government in their work The Israel Lobby and US Foreign Policy wade into these waters. Rev. Dr. Jeremiah A. Wright, Jr., retired pastor of the Trinity United Church of Christ in Chicago definitely fulfills the criteria of anti-Semite. Anti-Semitism can hardly be relegated to a small fringe group when a presidential candidate attends a church that publishes and praises the Hamas Charter in a church periodical.

This emerging wave of anti-Semitism is another threat to freedom, to western way of life. What is a person dedicated to freedom do when he or she hears the vile propaganda that wants to choke Israel out of existence and demeans Jews with sarcasms as the "Chosen" (read "entitled") people. The New Anti-Semitism is another threat to the Jewish people's existence.

So here in Vermont, on Church Street America, it is time for a Golem—a Golem who can save the Jews and every other person who believes in the rights of the individual.

A Jew who speaks out loudly against anti-Semitism walks a narrow line between offense and defense. In the past, Jews who have stood up to anti-Semitism or Dhimmitude have been smacked down. Holding one's tongue, by contrast, carries the hope that the hate will go away if one does not draw attention. Self-censorship, this mincing of words so as not to offend the majority, has led to Jews fighting among themselves. Sooner or later, prejudice, if not confronted, will win.

In making this art and these statements, I walk that narrow line. I do not want to offend. My objective is to draw attention, to educate, and to stimulate reflection. Will some people be offended? Probably. Am I denigrating any religion or race? No.

Everyone has the choice to interpret his or her religion as justifying hatefulness or not. When I am judgmental, it is of those who choose to shut off compassion and to perpetuate hate.

Many peace-and-justice organizations in the United States and Europe have become infected with an anti-Israel viciousness that slides into anti-Jew bias. Their partiality leads them away from advocating for peace and toward being a booster club for the Palestinian armies and terrorists. They have lost sight of the fact that to gain peace both sides of a conflict must be drawn in and heard. This conflict between Israel and Palestine is not just any tribal conflict. It pulls in historical animosities developed over thousands of years by Christian, Muslim and, more recently, Hindu and Jewish leaders. This conflict is a toxic soup of economic, political, religious, and racist interests. We cannot turn to righteous crusaders spurting sacrificial solutions to solve the conflict. Those with self-interest and hard bargaining skills must be trusted not to spread blame, but get to tough compromises that in the end no one will be completely happy with.

What lies at the core of our impulse to choose sides, and our "us against them" mentality, is the instinct to survive. There is another will: the desire to create and express a personal uniqueness. Hope for the respect of personal expression inspires this work, along with anger and the need for laughter.

This series of prints and commentary, *The Golem of Church Street,* starts with an outcry against anti-Semitism in my own neighborhood. That historic prejudice is returning, making one of its cyclic visits back to civilization—not that it has ever completely left.

This work is not a radical call or even political, per se. It is simply an insistence on the continuation of the Jewish people. It is a call for freedom from persecution and for the continued sovereignty of a Jewish state. It is a renewed call for the demise of anti-Semitism and a rejection of bigotry in general.

I offer these words and images with respect for my ancestors and the dignity with which they faced the challenges of their time, challenges I did not have to face myself. I am angry at old allies who have abandoned the Jews at this time: the fundamentalist Left, a group of people so blinded by their ideals for a socialist society that they cannot see the reality on the ground and the suffering of all people. By jumping on the anti-Semitism bandwagon, the fundamentalist Left imperil the well-being of Jews all over the world with an increasingly open disregard. This art reflects my reaction to the institutionalized goal of the extermination of Jews, last strongly incarnated in the policies of the Nazi party. When the Egyptian Muslim Brotherhood and the Grand Mufti of Palestine teamed up with Adolf Hitler sixty-two years ago, they shared a hatred for Jews and the British. This ideology and purpose informs the most rabid totalitarian Mid-Eastern regimes and jihadists.

My art is an extension of my nervous system, and my nervous system reacts to the sensory and abstract world around me. People who know me say, 'In the past you never identified so strongly with being a Jew,' and 'You never seemed to be so into Israel as you are now.' That is rue. The blatant recurrence of historic Jew-hatred today shocks me into reaction.

How Jewish did one have to feel in 1492, to be told to convert or die at the hands of the Inquisition? How Jewish did you have to feel in Europe at the end of the nineteenth century to be limited in your career or tortured by a pogrom? How Jewish did you have to feel in order to be carted off by Hitler to a camp? And how Jewish will you have to feel to be beheaded in the twenty-first century? Curiously, no Jew-hater asks, 'How Jewish do you feel?'

The Golem of Church Street is an expression of who I am. I see the other side, and the other side of the other side. I see the inversions, a world turned upside down. I see the donkey riding the man, and I see the peace dove with bloody talons. I look over my shoulder, and I see my would-be protector about to attack me. I look in front of me, and I see that the man reaching out to help me was recently my enemy.

The self-indulgent, self-righteous, and slanderous metaphors of evil that are commonly used against Israel and Jews today only veil the hatefulness and evil in the accuser. The Golem is the

Shiva of the Jews--the Creator and Destroyer--the loving and the ruthless. To deny either side is to be controlled by it.

To be whole in the Palestinian-Israeli conflict is to share blame, shame, and forgiveness. Not just between Palestinians and Jews but among all the players in world's power structure

Maybe the Middle East question so resists solutions because it mirrors that eternal human conflict between Cain and Abel, between altruism and survival, between self and other.

When the Palestinian voice is considered to carry the message of the destruction of the Jewish state, or when the Jewish message is the complete disenfranchisement of the Palestinian people, no integration is possible on either side.

David Sokol

2008

The Golem of Church Street

The Golem is the Jewish Superman/Frankenstein. The motivation for this Jew made of clay was not created out of scientific curiosity or self-serving ego. He was created, with dread and trembling, by a mystical Rabbi using Cabalistic power. The Rabbi who "fathered" the Golem did so with such trepidation because he knew that there was a stricture against man attempting to create life. Only God was great enough to create life. But in 16th century Prague, where this story originates, the Emperor was one of a long line of Jew killers. And this time it seemed the Emperor was going to exterminate the lot of them. The Rabbi reached into the formless cosmic mass and created life. Out of clay he formed a powerful life to do violence to those who would finally exterminate the Jewish people. The superhero/monster did protect the Jews and caused the Emperor to back down.

The Rabbi had to decide whether or not to give life to the creature. He wanted to save his Jews. The Jewish leader's spiritual studies, like Shakespeare's Prospero and Mary Shelley's Dr. Frankenstein, achieved for him powers over time and space. Over life itself. But what terrible consequences would ensue if man took God's role? This presents an eternal question especially to modern citizens with the technology of weaponry and genetics.

The Rabbi knew that no one but God could master life. The consequences of having a live Golem around were unpredictable. Many stories did tell that after the Golem protected the Jews he ran amok and killed innocent people. The Jews were saved but innocents were killed. Luckily there was a way for the Rabbi to "decommission" the Golem and stop his violence. This story shows the deep Jewish ambivalence toward violence.

Later Christianization and anti-Semitic versions of the story have the Golem creation motivated by Jewish greed and ambition. But the original story reflects a human dilemma about survival, not about greed.

What would you do? It is each person's choice whether to act in response to what he thinks is wrong. But often action's consequences are unintentional. Would you use violence to survive? Violence always hurts more than just the guilty. The celebration of a violent victory is at best ambivalent. The ugly part of humans comes out when rage, anger, and Golem strength is unleashed. But Golem is part of us. And if we do not accept him he will emerge without our will or control.

woodcut on paper
printed at sokolpress

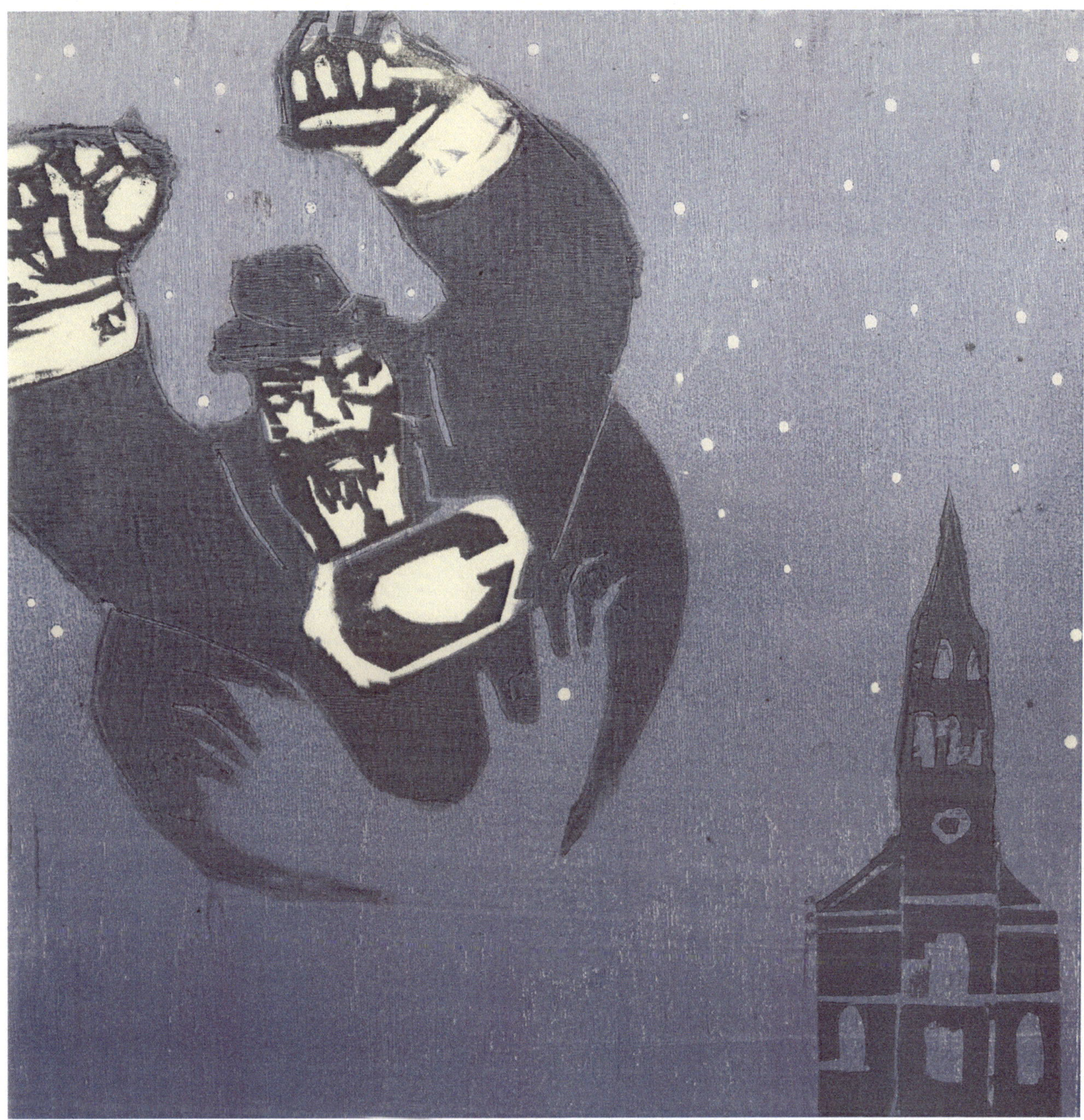

Dhimmitude

Jews and the Devil walk across the street …or else.

How many times have you heard that Jews and Muslims lived next to each other in the Arab world for thousands of years? They did so only under the Koranic institution of Dhimmitude. A Dhimmi is a Christian or Jew whom the Muslim community considers deserving of protection.

Muslims protected Dhimmis only as long as the Dhimmis functioned as second-class citizens and followed the special rules laid down by Islam. These rules included the payment of special taxes, restrictions on building, a ban on complaining about one's place in society, and the rule commanding Jews to walk to the left of a Muslim because that is where the Devil and the Jews belong. These rules were commonly enforced around the Arab world.

At a meeting of Arab, Palestinian, Israeli, and American leaders in Annapolis in November 2007, Arab representatives would neither touch nor sit near Tzipi Livni, the foreign minister of Israel. They were demonstrating what they considered her Dhimmitude. Breaking the rules of Dhimmitude has led to murder, rape, and loss of one's right to practice Judaism. Almost all Jews (850,000 since 1948) have now escaped from life in Arab lands, and they have thereby escaped the degrading state of Dhimmitude.

Yes, there have been individual moments of friendship between Jews and Muslims in the Arab world. It would certainly happen more often in an equal democracy. But radical Muslims are apparently infuriated and, indeed, feel personally humiliated when Jews dare to presume equality and to live outside the "protection" of Muslims. Real equality between Mid Eastern Muslim and Jew will be something new and will be even harder to achieve than real equality between white and black. Denying that deep anti-Semitism exists in the Arab world is like denying that deep racism ever existed between whites and blacks.

dry point etching
on paper printed
at Studio 250

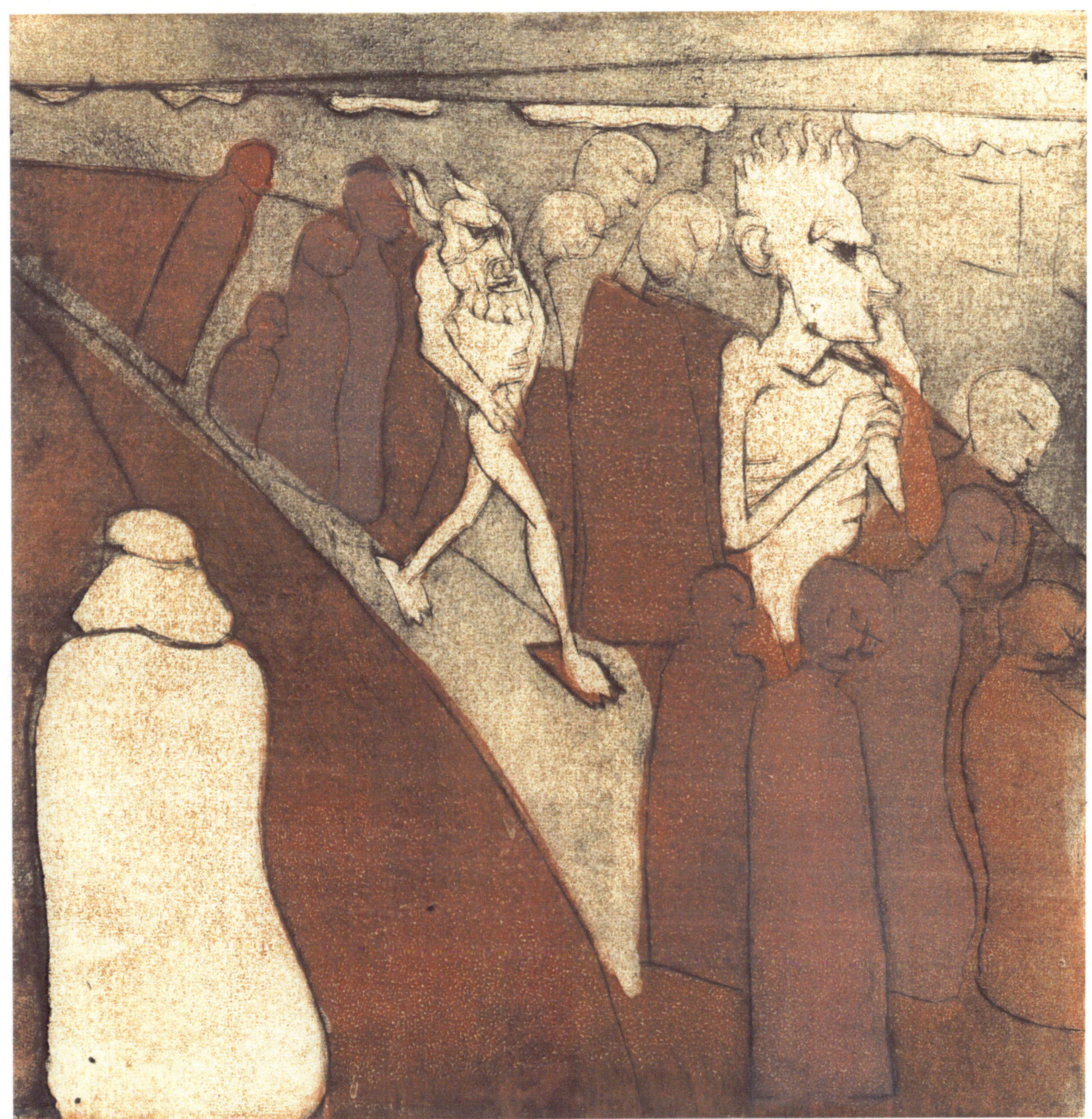

Sympathy for Other's Sorrows

Clare Booth Luce, wife of the onetime publisher of *Time* magazine and a congresswoman, reported a frank conversation that she once had with a Jewish friend. Luce said, "I must admit being positively bored by all this talk of the Holocaust and its constant repetition of Jewish suffering." The Jewish friend replied, "I know just how you feel. I feel exactly the same way about the Crucifixion."

copperplate etching
on paper printed
at Ningyo Press

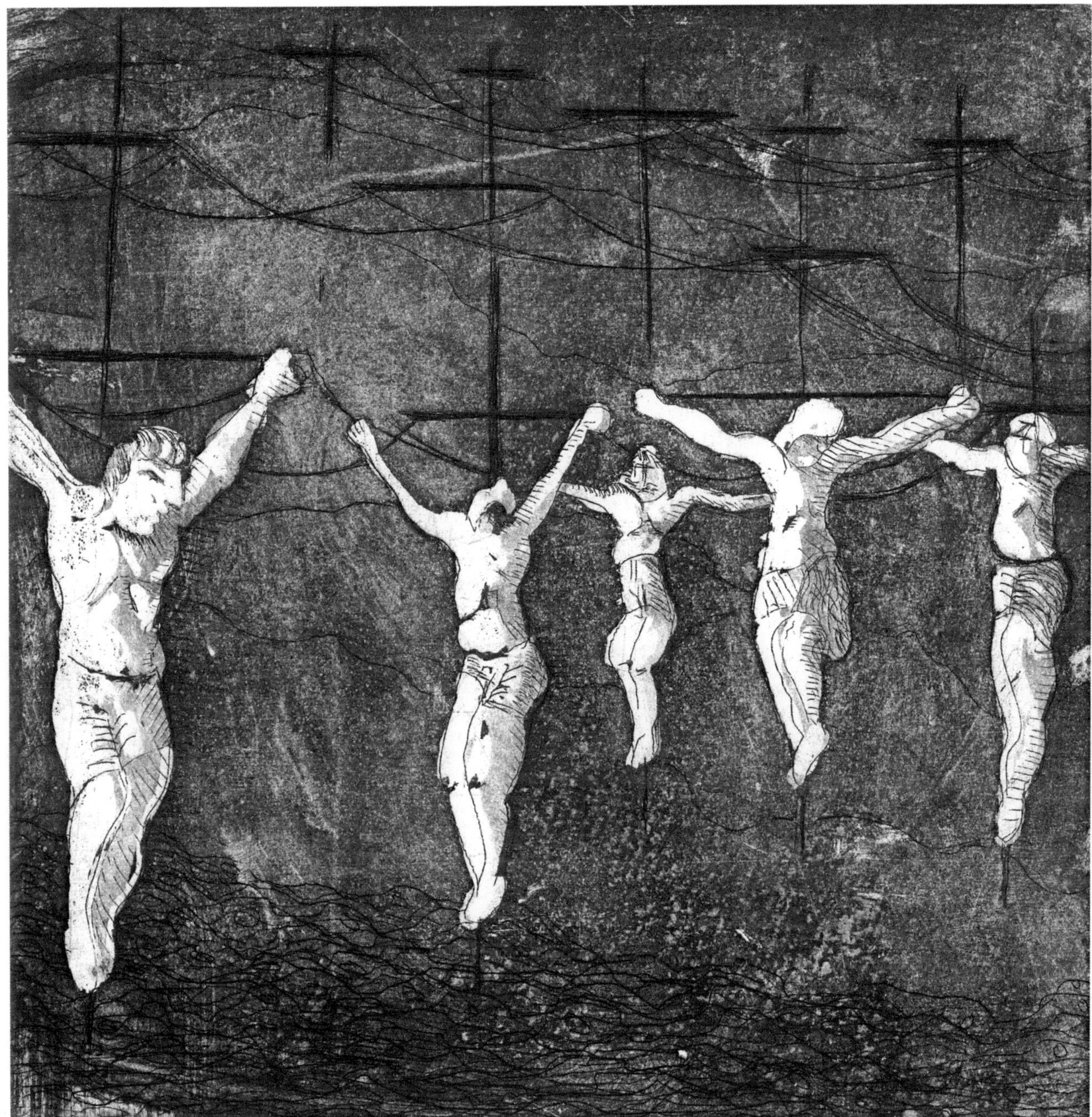

The Story of Grandma Sophie and Her Kids

Grandma Sophie was fourteen when she met the immigration officer on Ellis Island. She had not come to the United States in order to one day play golf or drive a Cadillac. She came to live a life where her family would not be abused.

Her sons took some bloody noses from anti-Semites, but they grew up and did not complain.

Her boys discovered the medicine Interferon. They helped send Project Mercury into space. They coordinated weapons for NATO member country arsenals, protecting America and Western Europe. Now her children and grandchildren are accused of being "disloyal" to the United States because they support Israel.

reduction woodcut
on paper printed
at sokolpress

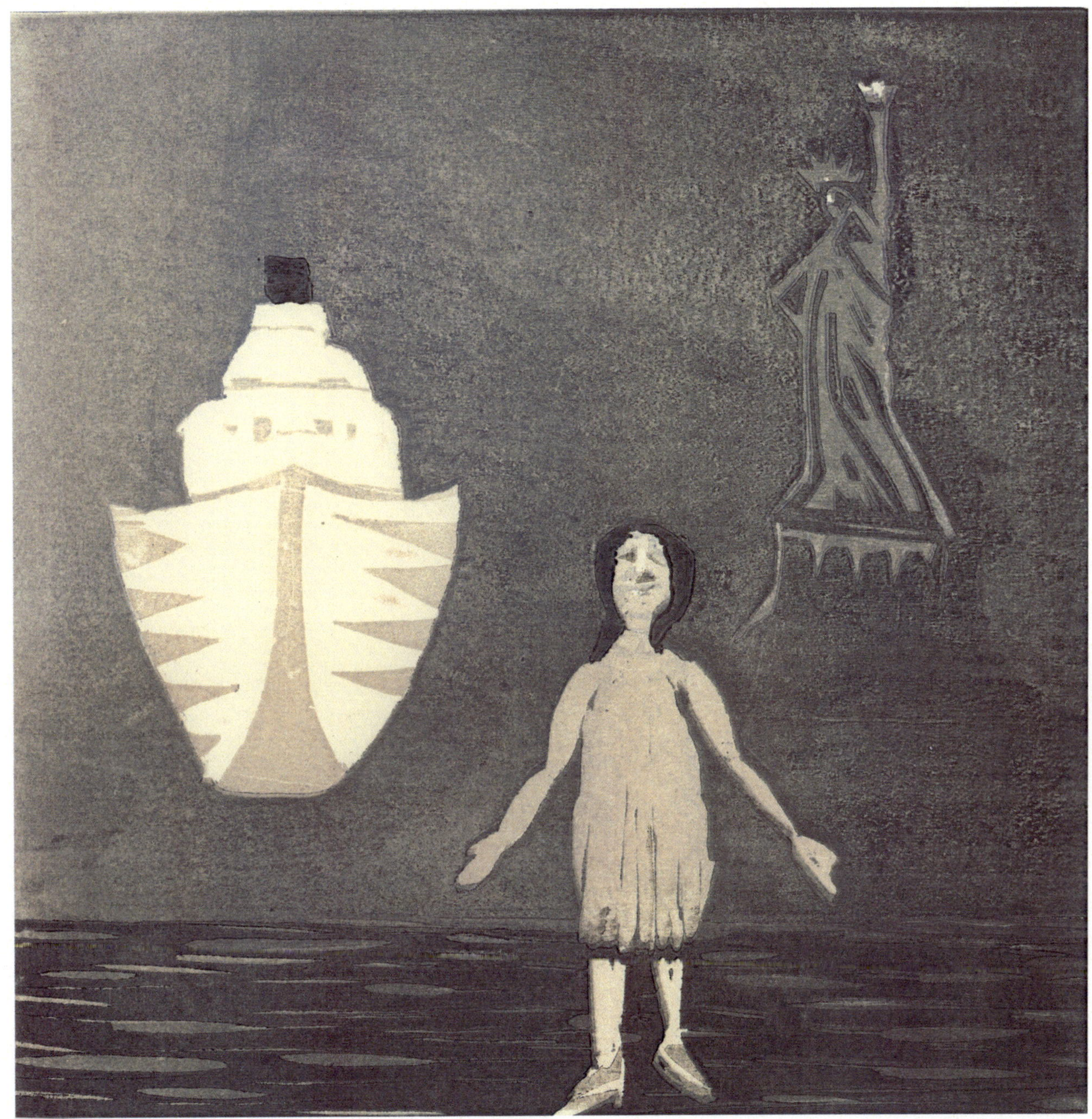

The Story of a War Hero and His Son

A retired lawyer tells this story from his childhood. When he was a little boy, his dad came home from World War II as an air force hero. He had flown missions over Germany and had gained quite a reputation in the community as a hero. When Dad took his son to the local golf club to teach him how to play, they were greeted with congratulations and thanks for his war contribution. They were also turned away from the property because "very sorry, but Jewish people are not permitted to play at this club." The boy never forgot.

dry point and monoprint
on paper printed
at sokolpress

18

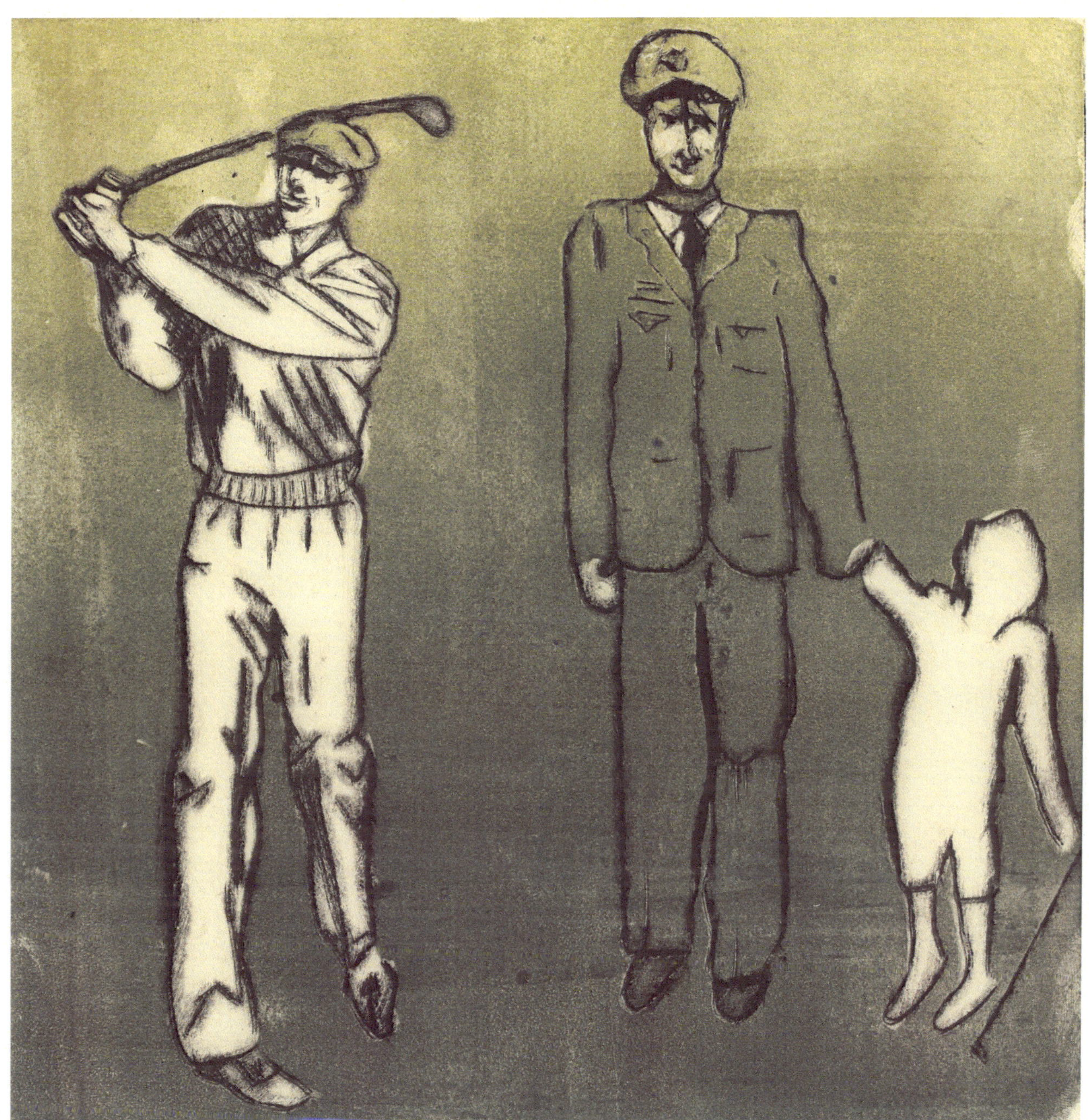

Papa (and I do not mean Ernest Hemingway)

Karl Marx hated those who disagreed with him. He hated a lot.

There is a core of Jew haters, many of them, like Marx, Jews themselves, who would agree with his following statements:

"What is the Jew's foundation in our world? Material necessity, private advantage."

"What is the object of the Jew's worship in this world? Usury. What is his worldly God? Money."

"Money is the zealous one god of Israel."

"The bill of exchange is the Jew's real God."

"What is the worldly religion of the Jews? It is the petty haggling of the hawker."

"The social emancipation of the Jew is the emancipation of society from Judaism."

monoprint on paper
printed at sokolpress

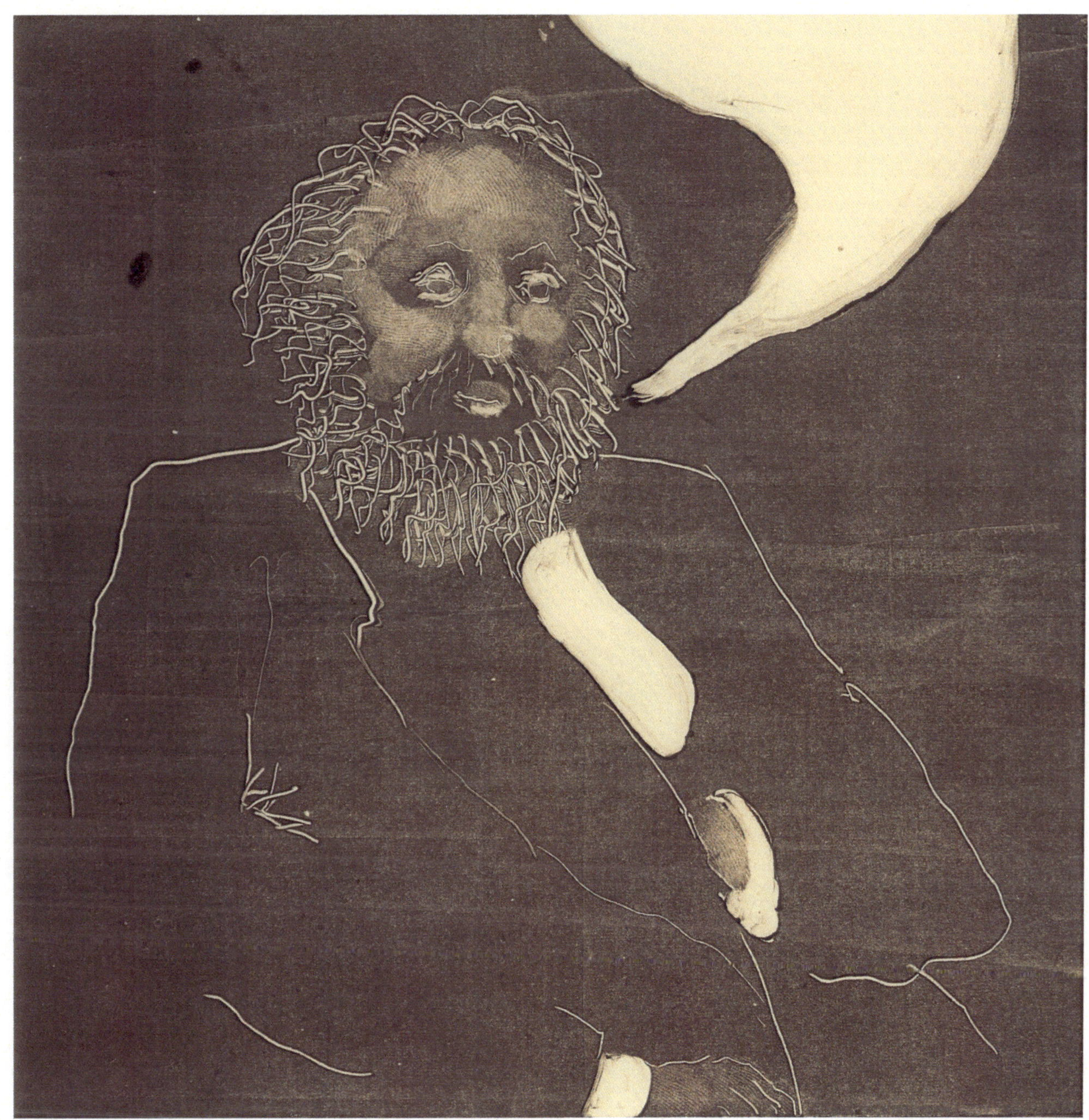

Dealing with False Idols-Blowing up the Buddha

In 2001, the Taliban of Afgahanistan blew up a two thousand year old giant statue of the Buddha. This Buddha was the biggest draw for tourists in the country. Any belief other than their own is not tolerated by the Taliban.

The last two Jews in Afghanistan were whipped with electric cables and beaten with rifle butts and told to convert. "Not for a million dollars" was their response. One died on the synagogue floor. The other is still searching for a four-hundred-year-old Torah stolen by an inmate now residing at Guantanamo.

dry point, monoprint
and ink line drawing
on paper printed at
sokolpress

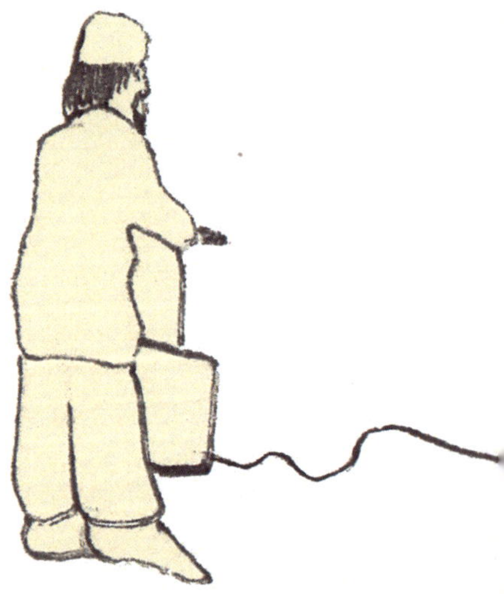

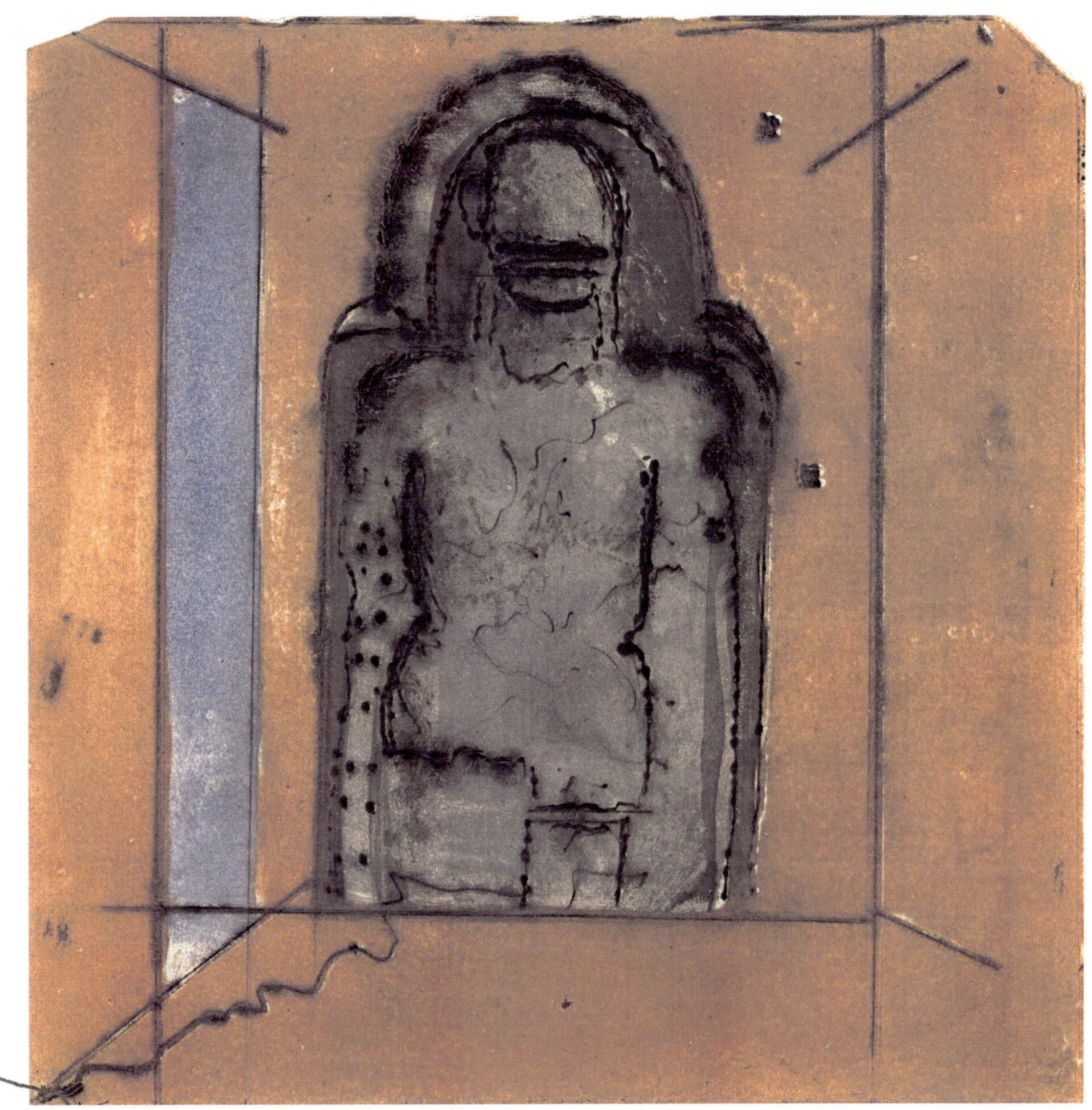

The Story of the Jewish Barn

A woman recalls a memory from her childhood in 1963. In the pastoral
hills outside Burlington, Vermont, neighbors burned down the Jew's barn. The
family had not been there long, and everyone knew they were not welcome.
Theirs and the neighbor's children were not allowed to play together. No
one questioned that the fire was intentional, yet, of course, no one was held
responsible. The Jews got the message and moved out six months later.

woodcut on paper
printed at Ningyo Press

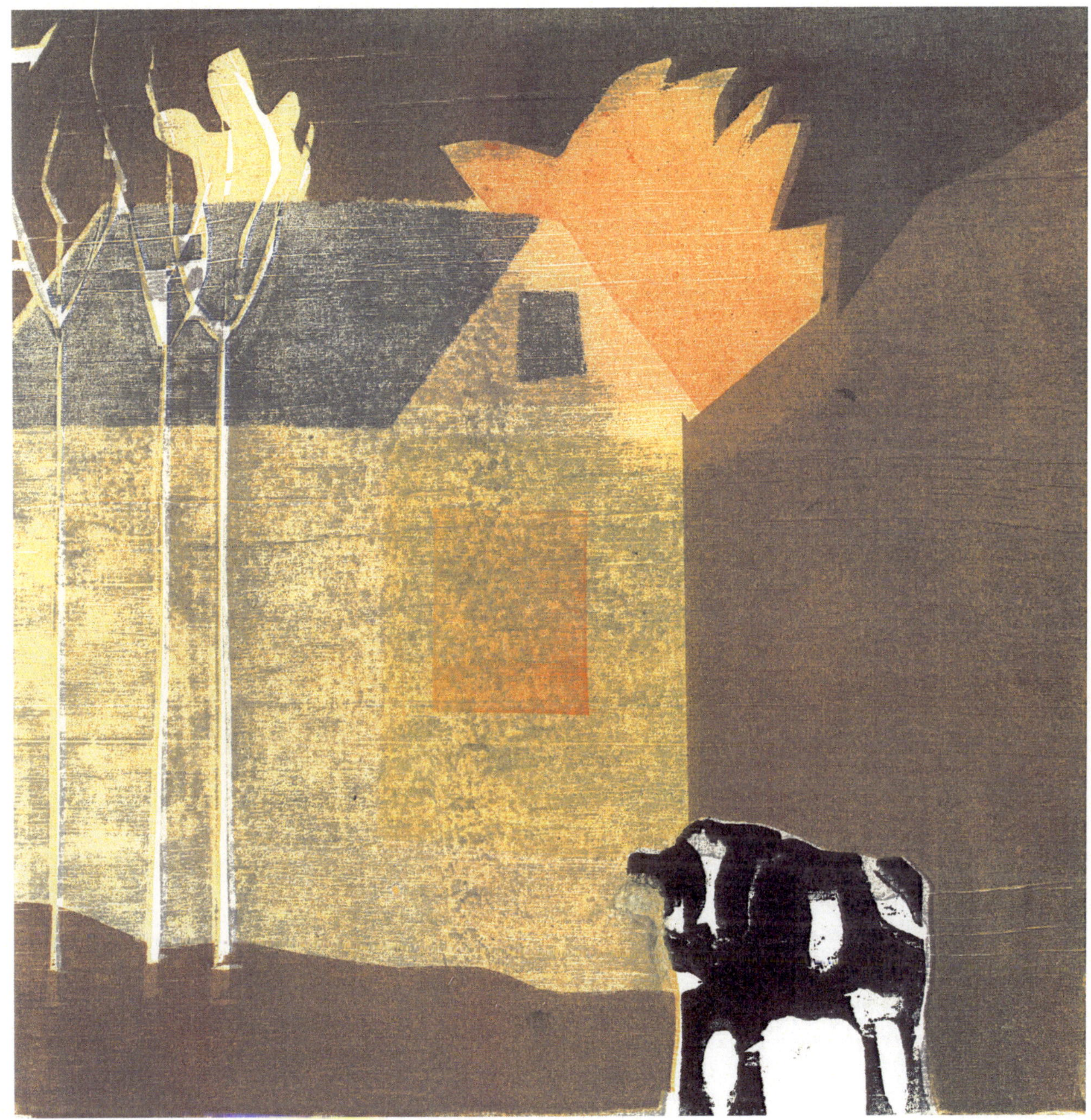

Schmeered

"When people criticize Zionists they mean Jews, you are talking anti-Semitism."

Martin Luther King
1968 Speech at Harvard

Even though many people who oppose the Jewish state of Israel do not consciously "hate Jews", they participate in functional anti-Semitism. They discriminate against the Jewish people by denying them the right to be themselves.

They single out Israel as "colonialist", but ignore numerous other governments that could be more accurately accused.

They call Israel racist, but ignore the Israeli commitment to equality of all Israeli citizens and ignore the Israeli commitment to the sovereign state of Palestine.

They accuse Israel of stealing land, but ignore the property and monetary losses of 850,000 Jewish refugees forced from Arab countries. They also ignore the practice of land acquisition after war by other countries in the world.

They hold the preposterous accusation that Israel is an apartheid state. Apartheid references one comparison and that is to the old South African regime. The differences between the two are fundamentally vast. When Israeli human rights abuses are brought up they are brought up in an artificial context that ignores the difficult situation of a country surrounded by those wanting to extinguish it. Comparisons to extreme human rights abuses around the world are absurd. Crimes occur in any country that is at war. Israel has a court system in place to try to deal with human rights abuses and allows public protest on any issue.

transfer monoprint on
paper printed at
sokolpress

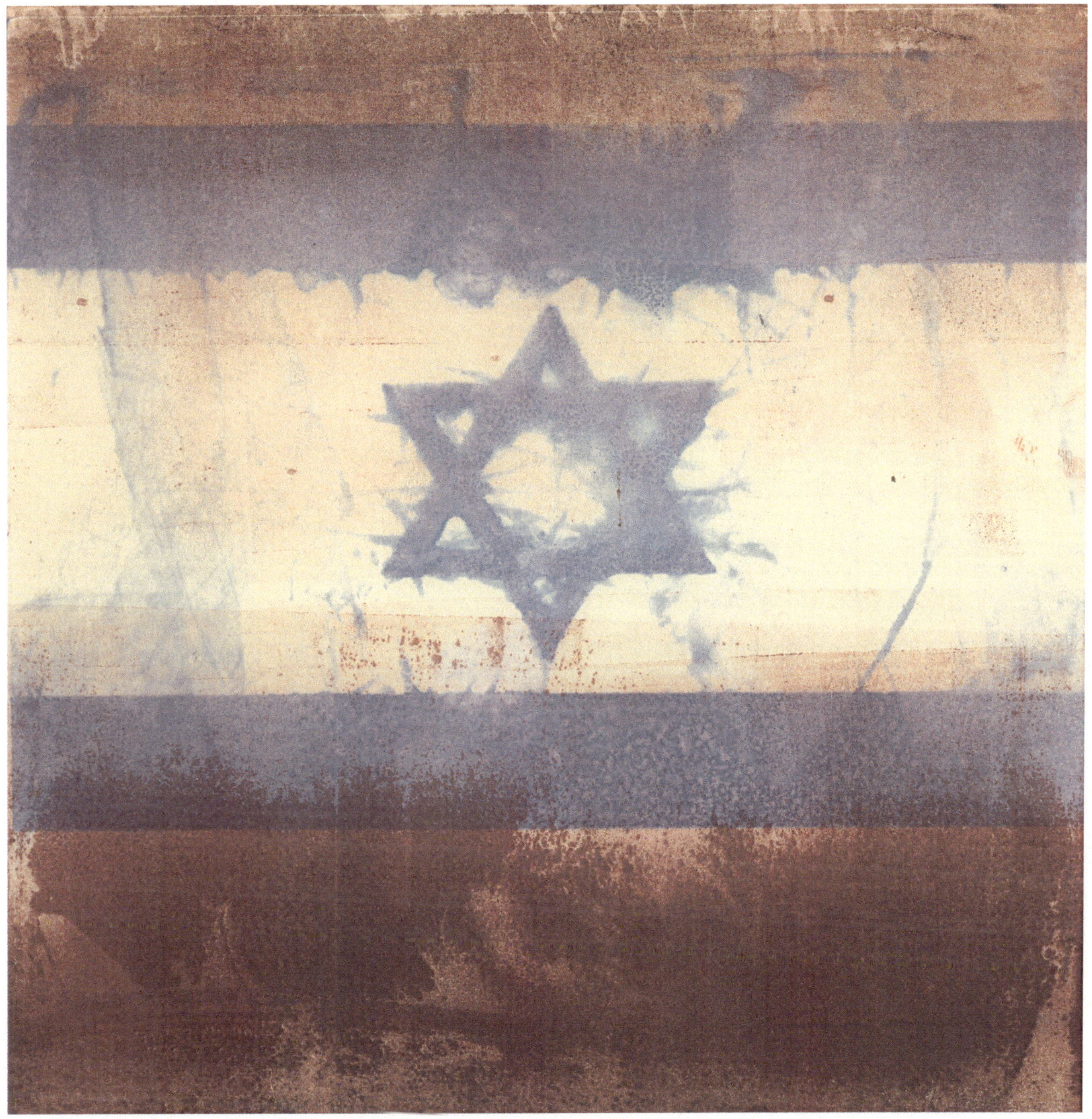

Ridden by Donkeys

The true believers have become the beasts of burden whom the more intelligent donkeys ride. When Jews defend themselves, they are said to be committing atrocities. When Arabs detonate bombs, they are said to be driven to it by the Jews. Who could believe this nonsense?

Some Jews carry the donkey of hate for Israelis. Why? Do they feel somehow guilty for not really belonging with the Gentiles? Or maybe turning against the all-too-human failures of their own tribe makes them feel especially self-righteous. Maybe they say to themselves, "Not me! I am one of the good ones." I don't know. These seem like weak interpretations for such screwed up hatred toward Israel in such a complex situation.

But Gentiles are part of this crowd, too. Some devout pre-Vatican II holdouts know they are no longer allowed to say "Christ-killers" out loud, but they can still dish out the smears every bit as well as their anti-Semitic ancestors. They still carry the donkey of political anti-Semitism for a church that no longer needs it. The brightest Christian leaders have partially undone anti-Semitism. But the fundamentalist left still makes available a niche for practitioners of that old-time religion. They sing the sweet peace-and-justice song calling for the end of th Jewish state.

The new version of anti-Semitism carries the donkey of "political correctness." This Jew-hating is "not racist"--it is said to be, in fact, "anti-racist," because they consider Zionism to be racism. Any anti-racist worth his or her salt, they maintain, must be against the Zionists. So it's open season on Israel.

Perhaps the most catastrophic outcome of the donkey mentality is purity. Purity is the logical outcome of the inability to accept our two-sided nature. Every totalitarian terrorist group has pushed the ideal vision of a kingdom on earth where all that is impure is overcome by a particular system or religion. Those systems always turn toxic.

Instead of people riding donkeys, the donkey rides the people. The donkeys are the leaders.

woodblock on paper
printed at sokolpress

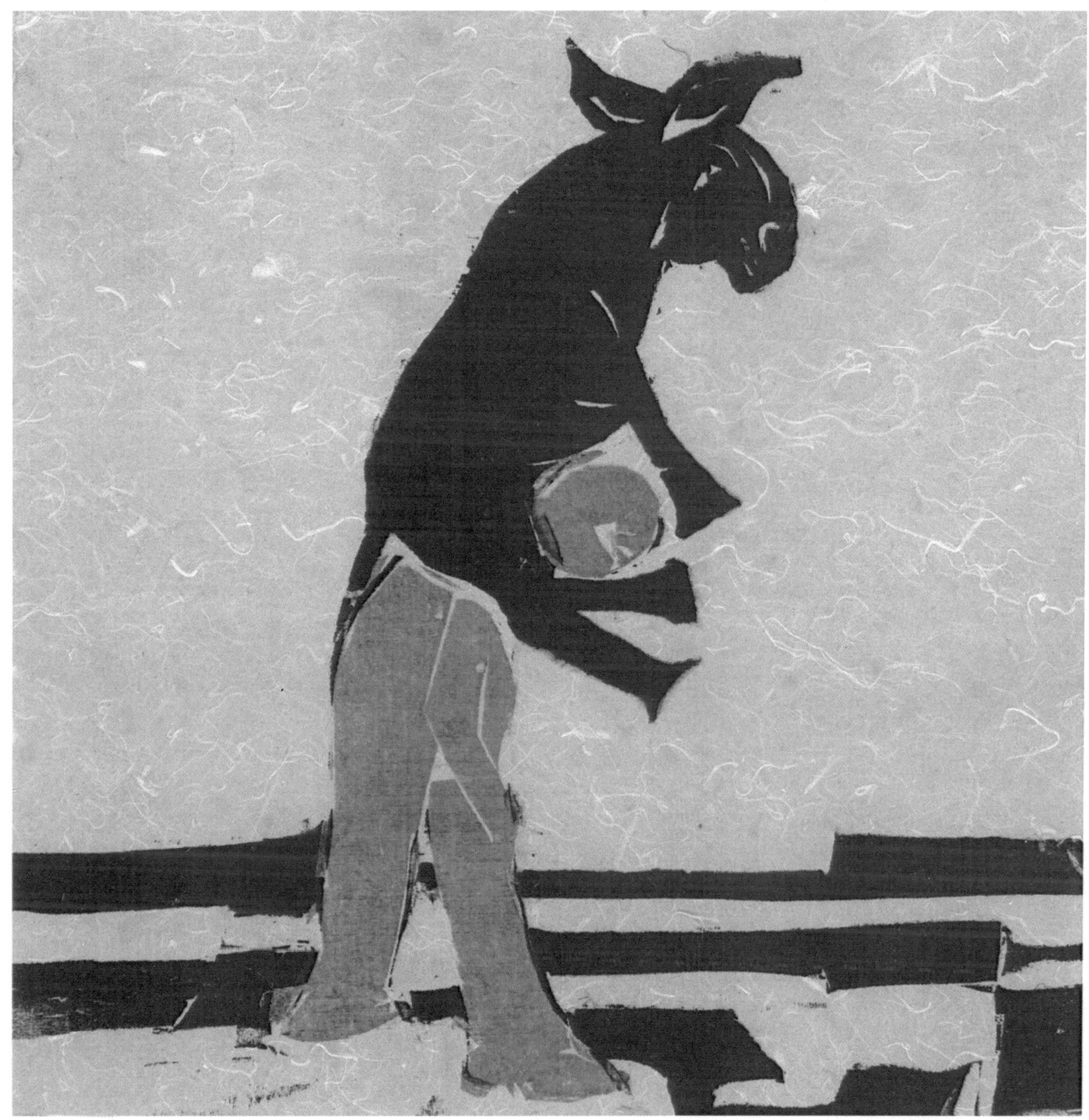

City of Fortune Becomes the City of Fear

October 26 and 27, 2007 the Old South Church in Boston rented space to the Sabeel Conference, hosted by the Sabeel Ecumenical Liberation Theology Center for a conference entitled "The Apartheid Paradigm in Palestine-Israel" with keynote speaker Archbishop Desmond Tutu. Rev. Nancy S. Taylor said the renting the sanctuary to Sabeel represented an idea that is "at the heart of a free and vital democratic nation." The executive director of Boston's Jewish Community Relations Council defended Sabeel's free speech rights, but also denounced the conference as "an effort to demonize the state of Israel."

According to a poll commissioned by the Joshua Fund, as of April 2008, 82% of U.S. Protestants and Catholics surveyed felt they had "a moral and Biblical obligation to support Israel and pray for peace in Jerusalem." The Old South Church represents another wing of the Christian church. These are upper class do-good believers who feel that giving voice to the underdog even if that voice is twisted and hate filled is the fair thing to do. If it walks like an anti-Semite, talks like anti-Semite you can bet it is an anti-Semite.

Blame the Jews and burn down the town. This has been going on for centuries. Most of the Christian Germans on the night of November 10, 1938 were not sitting up hating Jews. In fact many were crying as they looked out their windows all over Germany and watched shattering glass as 1000 synagogues were destroyed and tens of thousands of Jewish businesses smashed and pillaged and 30,000 Jewish men were taken to concentration camps. The trauma of holocaust was begun on this night by groups of Nazi thugs. It terrified not only Jews who made up less than 0.76% of Germany but terrified the whole civilian population. Economic hardship, fear, and a great country humiliated was the favorable situation in Germany to breed anti-Semitism. Soon after Kristallnacht, German Christian texts came out saying it was the Protestant will to be anti Semitic-Blame the Jews. The Government continued its message that it was healthy for Germans to hate Jews who were to blame for all Germany's hardships. In this traumatized atmosphere the underlying anti-Semitism was cultivated and spread like a highly infectious disease. The German people are recovering from this disease seventy years later.

etching and collage
on paper printed
at sokolpress

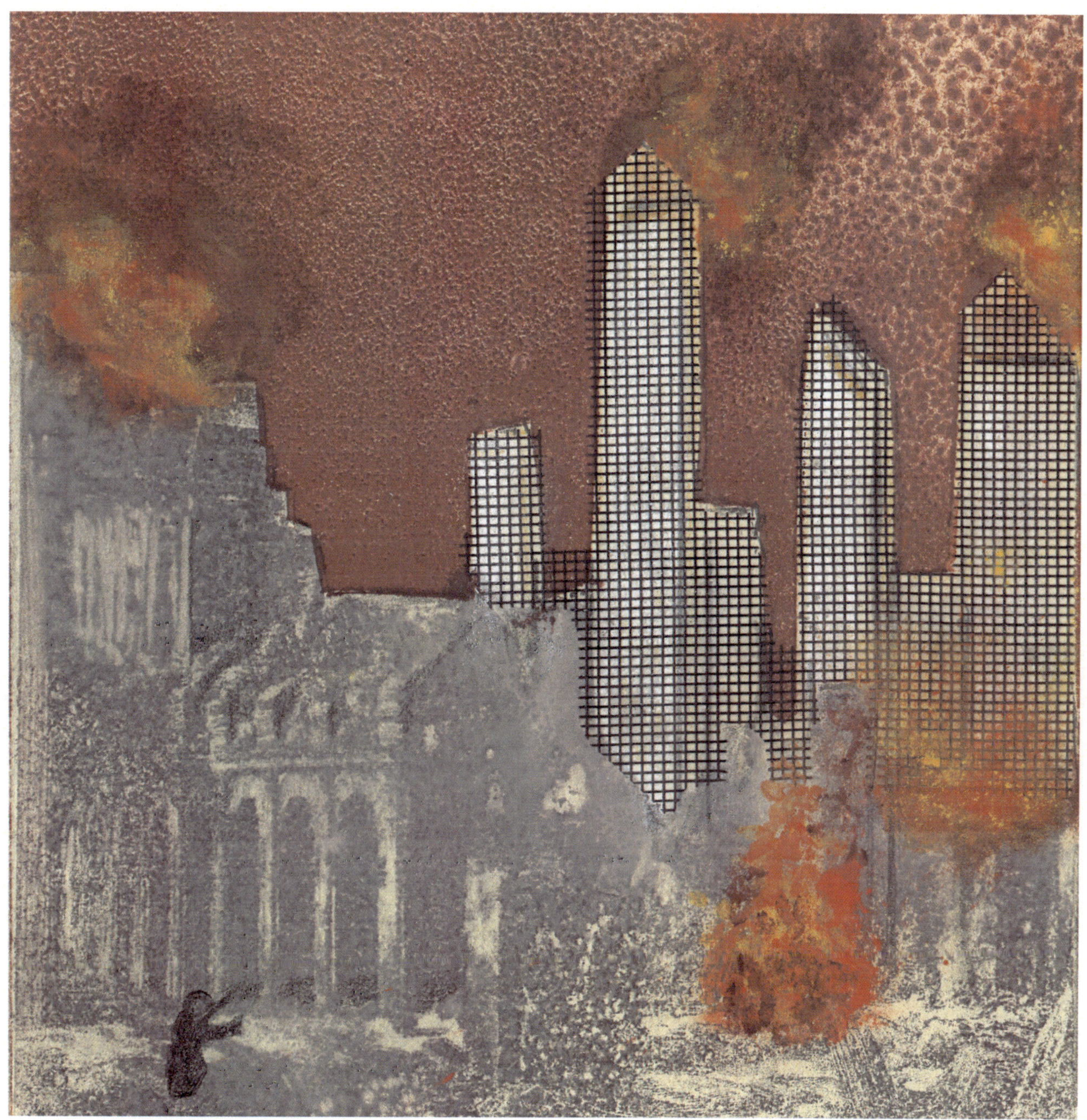

Farfour the Mighty Martyr Mouse

Farfour the Mouse was the star of Tomorrow's Pioneers, a Palestinian children's
TV show broadcast in 2007. Farfour was tricked, beaten and killed by Jews.
He achieved martyrdom, as all honorable children should strive to do. He was
replaced on the afternoon show by Naoul the Bee. Naoul teaches the children
that their highest aspiration should be to take vengeance, kill the Jews, and
join Farfour in martyrdom.

Here is some dialogue between a four-year-old girl and the and the host of a
Saudi Arabian talk show, speaking of Jews:

Doaa 'Amer (host of Iqraa-TV): Do you like them?

Basmallah: No

'Amer: Why don't you like them?

Basmallah: Because...

'Amer: Because they are what?

Basmallah: Because they are apes and pigs.

'Amer: Because they are apes and pigs. Who said they are so?

Basmallah: Our God.

'Amer: Where did he say this?

Basmallah: In the Koran.

Amer: That's right.

woodcut on paper
printed at sokolpress

The Islamic leader, the Grand Mufti Mohammad Amin Husseini of Jerusalem,
spent World War II in Berlin helping Adolf Hitler with the Nazi war effort.
Perhaps he brought back the educational philosophy of Hitler Youth to
Palestine?

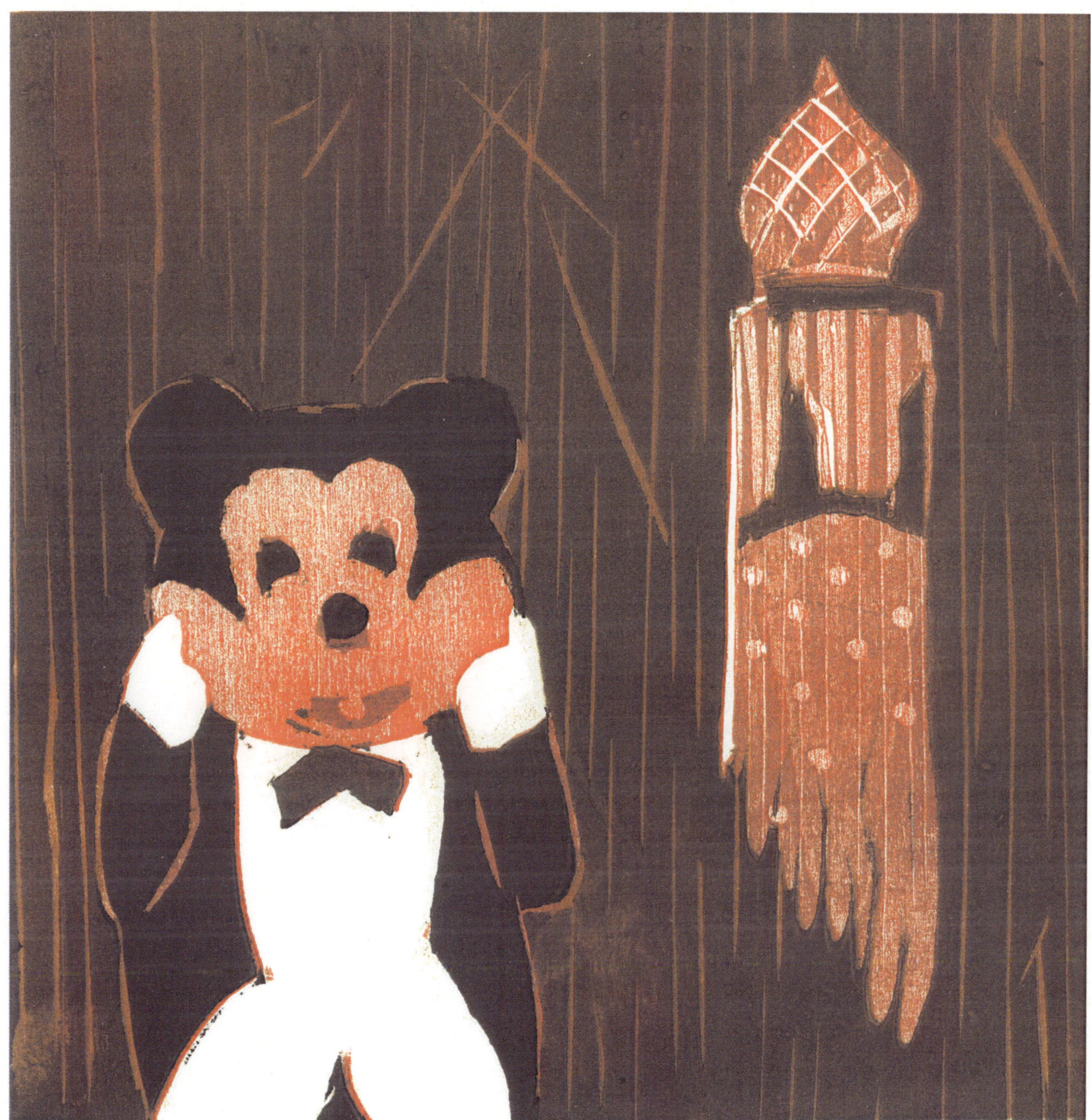

The Battle of Farfour-Institutionalized Child Abuse

Farfour the Mouse, a Palestinian television character, taught that death is more glorious than life and that nothing is more glorious than dying to kill a Jew.

"We must stop the propaganda to which Palestinian children are being exposed. That must be a priority for all people who care about children, who care about peace...these children deserve an education that instills respect for life and peace instead of glorifying death and violence. The videos we viewed at that Senate hearing were a clear example of child abuse.... Children were encouraged to see martyrdom and armed struggle and the murder of innocent people as ideals to strive for. It is disturbing to me on a human level, as a mother, it is disturbing to me as a United States Senator, because it basically, profoundly poisons the minds of these children."
Hillary Clinton, February 2007

Now, in 2008, Assoud, a Hamas version of Bugs Bunny, tells kids to "Eat the Jews".

copperplate etching
on paper printed
at Ningyo Press

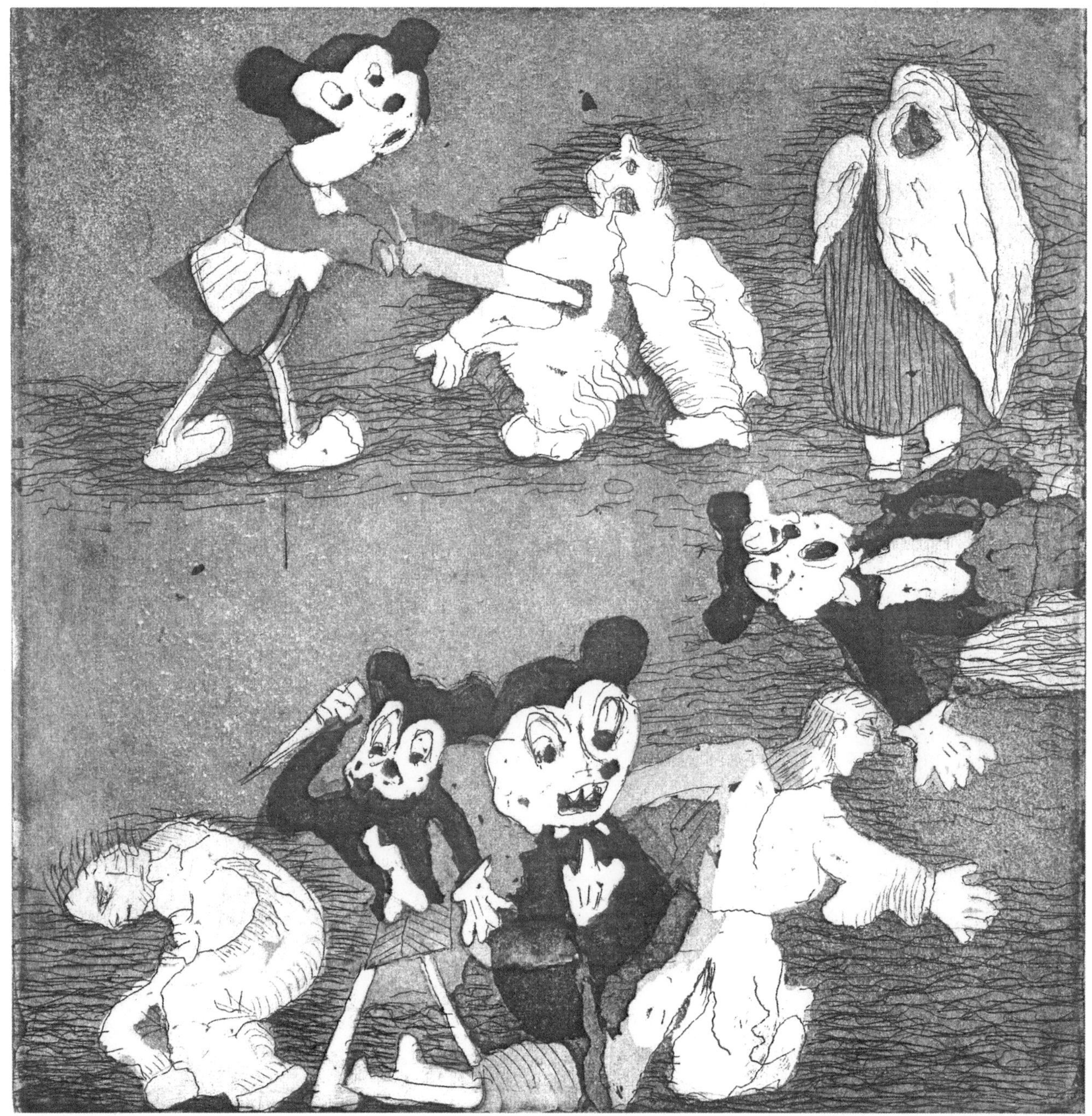

If Osama and Dr. Zawahiri Were Ben and Jerry's, Inc.

Ben and Jerry's represents the longing for a benign capitalism. The hip
innocence of its slogan "If it's not fun, why do it?" is what every kid wishes
was true.

Osama Bin Laden and Zawahiri's "corporation" devours death and destruction
the way they eat these ice cream cones, without grief, in fact with glee. You
can hear them say, "If it is not fun, why blow it up?"

monoprint and dry point
on paper printed
at sokolpress

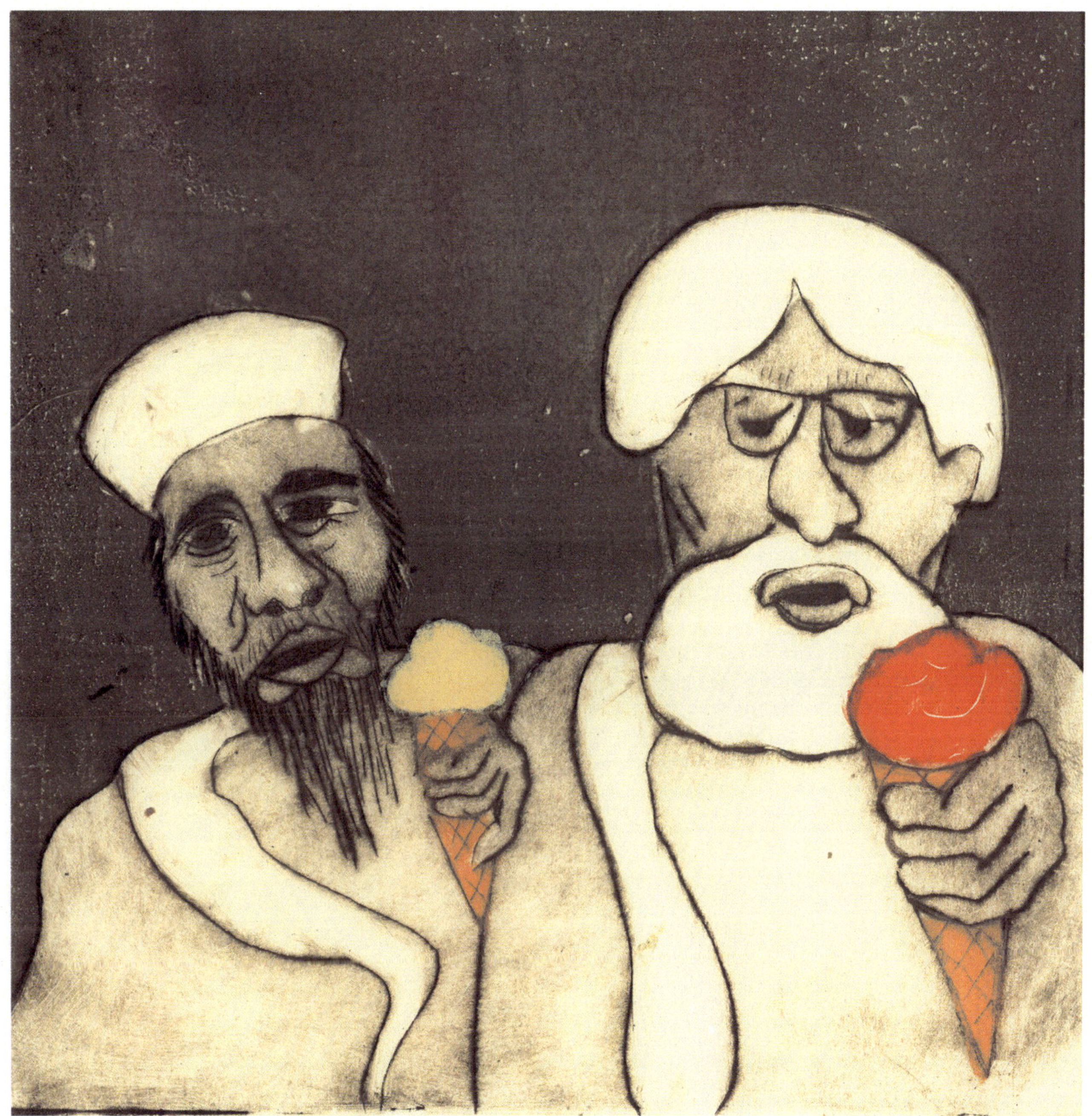

The A-list Terrorist - Portrait of Nasrallah

"If they [Jews] all gather in Israel, it will save us the trouble
of going after them world wide."
>Hassan Nasrallah, Secretary General of
>the terrorist group Hezbollah.

"I expressed concern that the state of Israel, by aggressive policies
towards its neighbors such as the war against Hezbollah and Lebanon, is,
in the long run, endangering the Jewish people, morally and physically."
>Robin Lloyd, a writer for *Vermont Peace
>and Justice Center News*

"If we searched the entire world for a person more cowardly, despicable,
weak and feeble in psyche, mind ideology and religion, we would
not find anyone like the Jew. Notice, I do not say the Israeli."
>Nasrallah as quoted in *The New Yorker*

"Hezbollah has set an example of resistance that could inspire
further struggles across the Middle East, potentially opening the
way for a secular left-wing alternative to take root and grow."
>John Von Camp in *Counterpunch*,
>a left-wing newsletter

woodcut with chine collé
printed at Ningyo Press

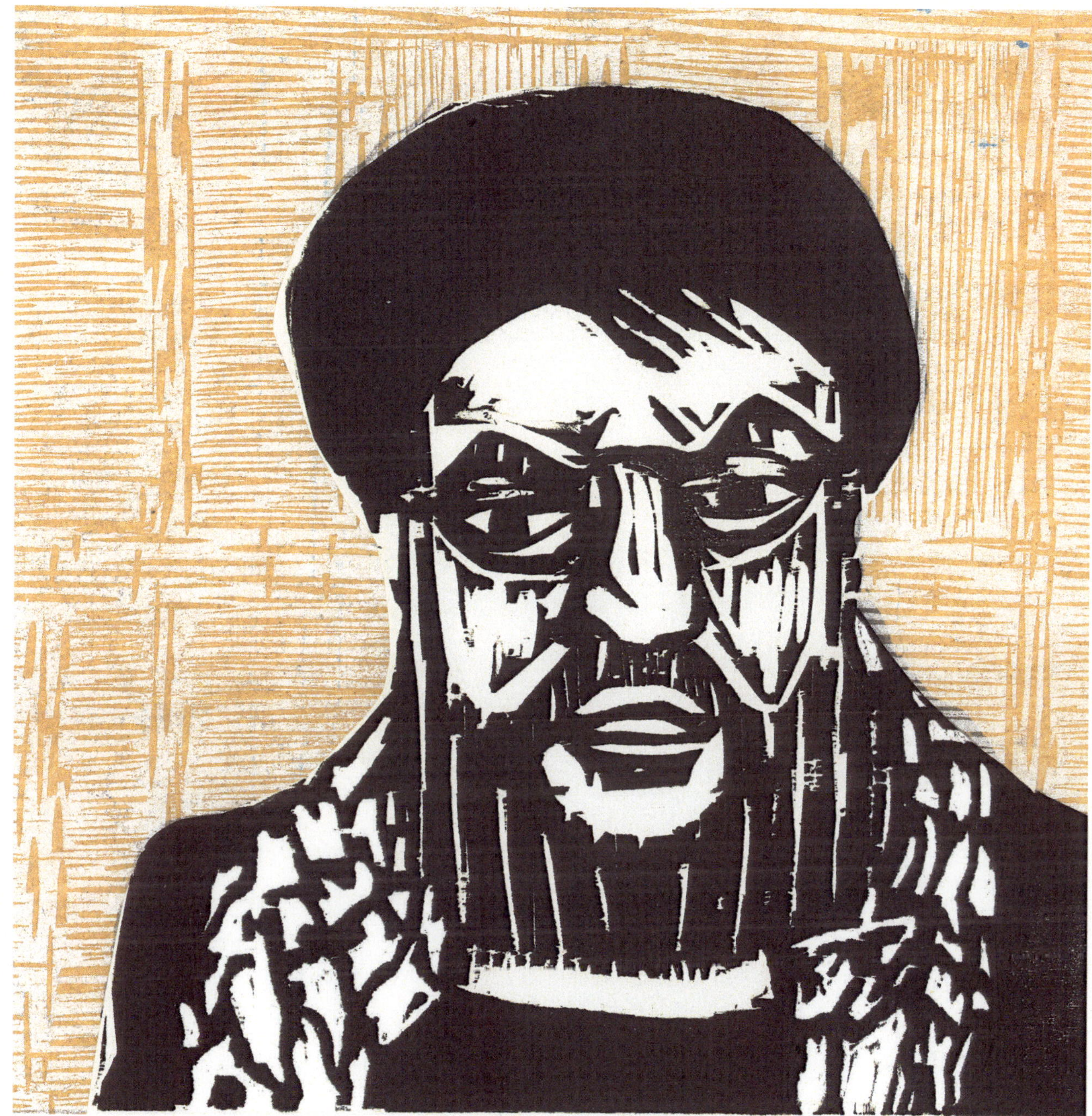

Puppets of the Fundamentalist Left

YOU CAN'T HAVE IT BOTH WAYS

You cannot say you are for a two-state solution

And support the advocacy of one state.

You cannot condemn violence

And then make excuses for Palestinian terrorism.

You cannot blame all violence on the Israeli "occupation" and at the same time say you are working toward a "just peace."

You cannot demonize one side with your bias and at the same time justify your distortion by saying the "world media" is biased.

You cannot ignore the deep hatred and desire to eradicate Israel and at the same time simply unilaterally demand a return to 1967 boundaries.

You cannot say you are for peace and at the same time cruelly encourage Palestinians to push for the impossible right of return of five million Arab descendants of refugees to Israel.

If you do this, you are not a peacemaker.

drawing transfer
monoprint with India ink
on paper printed
at sokolpress

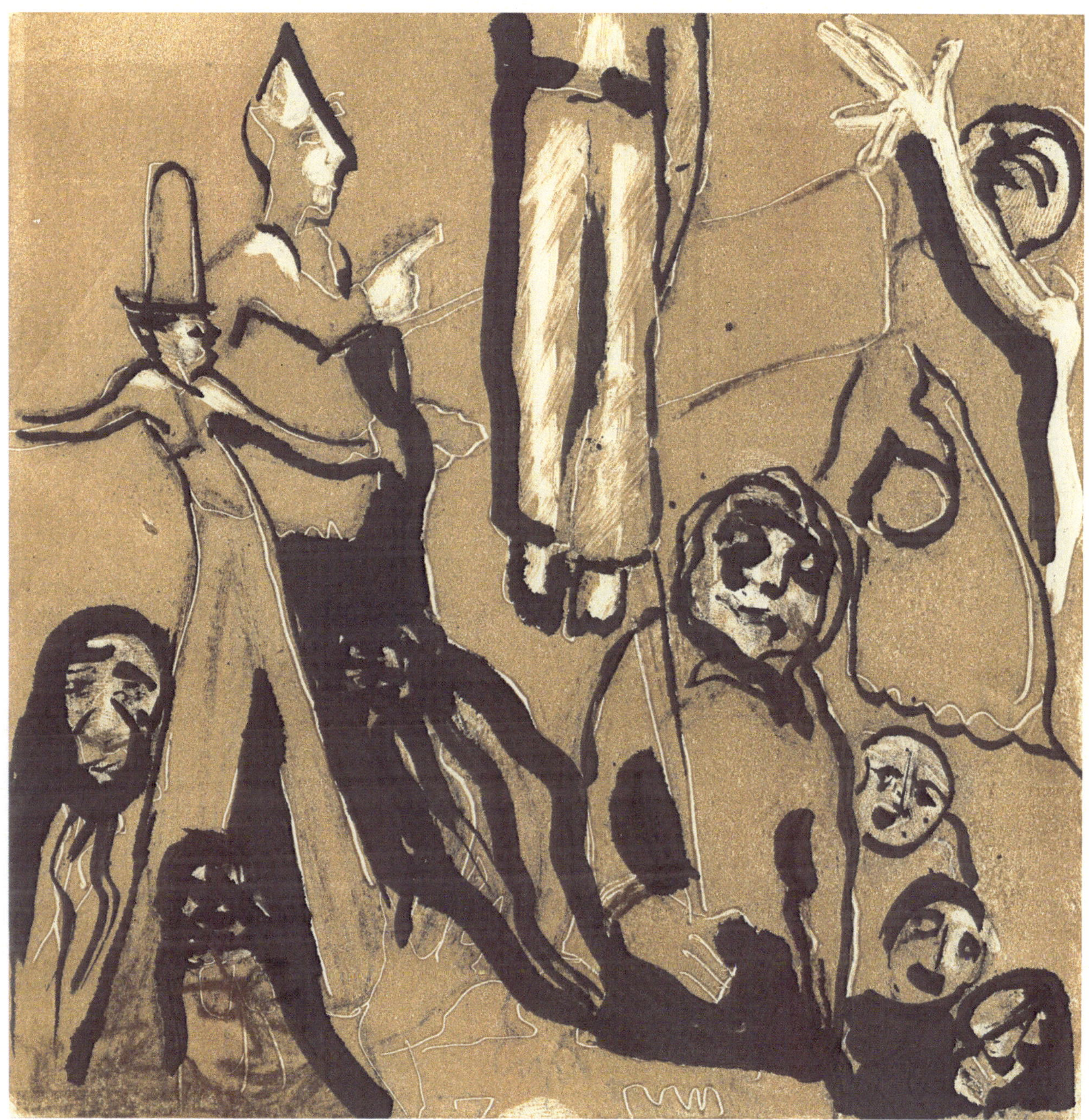

Code Words

Hey! Everyone come out from under your rocks and out of your holes.

It is okay to be anti-Semitic again. Just be sure you use the new code word:

"The Jewish Lobby"

dry point and monoprint
on paper printed
at sokolpress

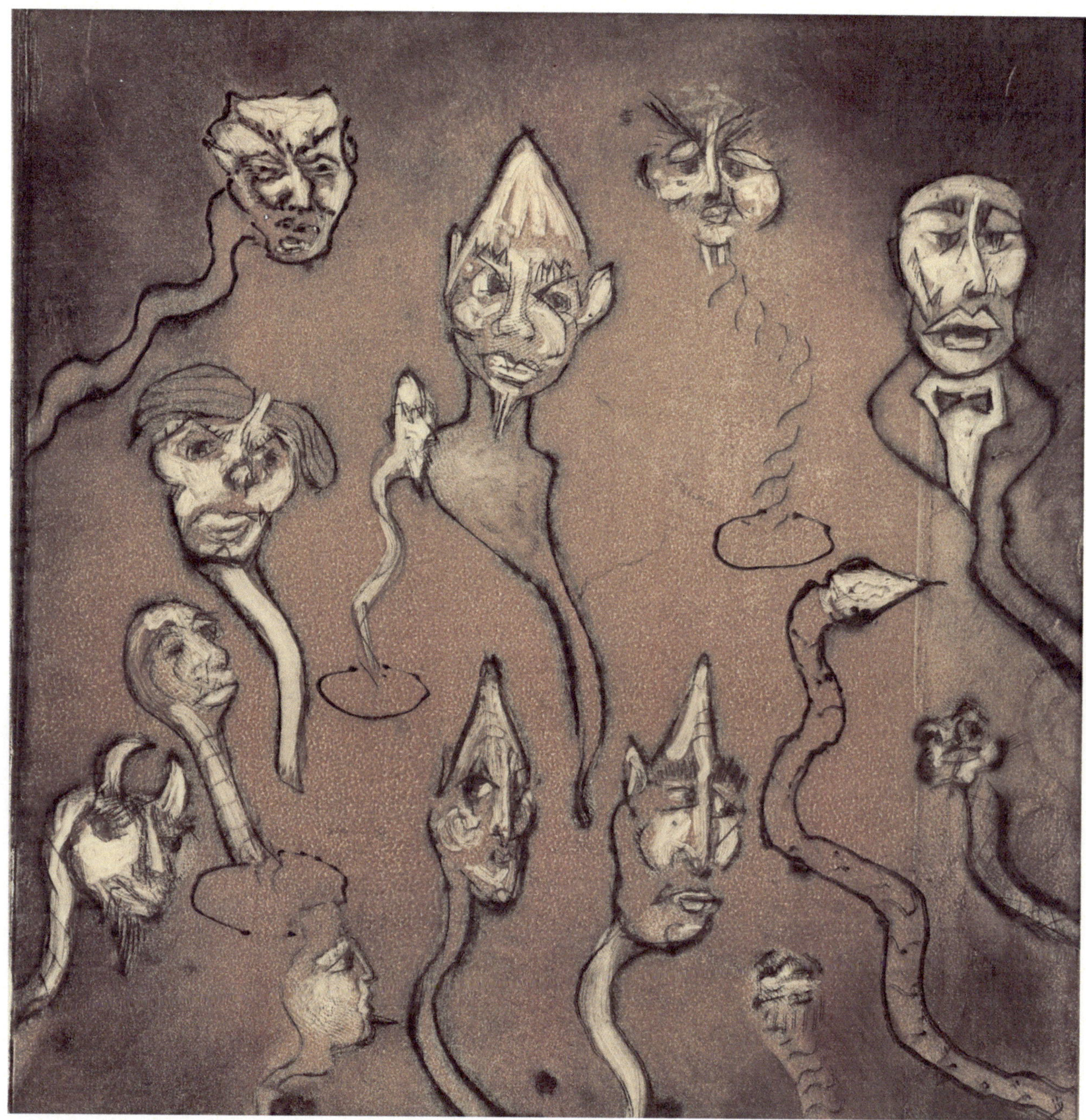

Selling Out for Peanuts

Jimmy Carter wrote a book called *Palestine: Peace Not Apartheid* blaming Israel for all the problems in the Israel-Palestine conflict. He said that the United States Congress is too influenced by American Jewish money.

Did you know that Carter has accepted millions of dollars in donations for his foundation and charitable projects from anti-Israel Arab individuals and groups?

He has taken big money from his "personal friend" Sheik Zayed bin Sultan al-Nahyan.

Harvard University returned two and one half million dollars in donations from the same man. They also refused to establish an academic chair in the name of Zayed's think tank. Their reason was that Zayed's money is so dirtied by his virulent anti-Semitism that no respectable organization would be associated with him. Jimmy keeps his money and called him a friend.

During the 1970s, Carter's peanut business was bailed out of financial trouble by an anti-Israel bank called BCCI. It was a crooked bank that has since dissolved, whose director once bragged that his bank was "the best way to fight the evil of Zionism."

After Carter's anti-Israel book was published, fourteen members of the the Carter Center's Board of Councilors resigned in protest of its dishonesty, inaccuracy, divisiveness, and bias. Overnight, Carter's supporters accused these human rights experts of being biased pro-Israelites. Any argument that opposes anti-Israel statements is put into that "Israel right or wrong crowd."

Jimmy is dependent on Arab money. Could this explain his distortion of truth against Israel?

dry point and monoprint
on paper printed
at sokolpress

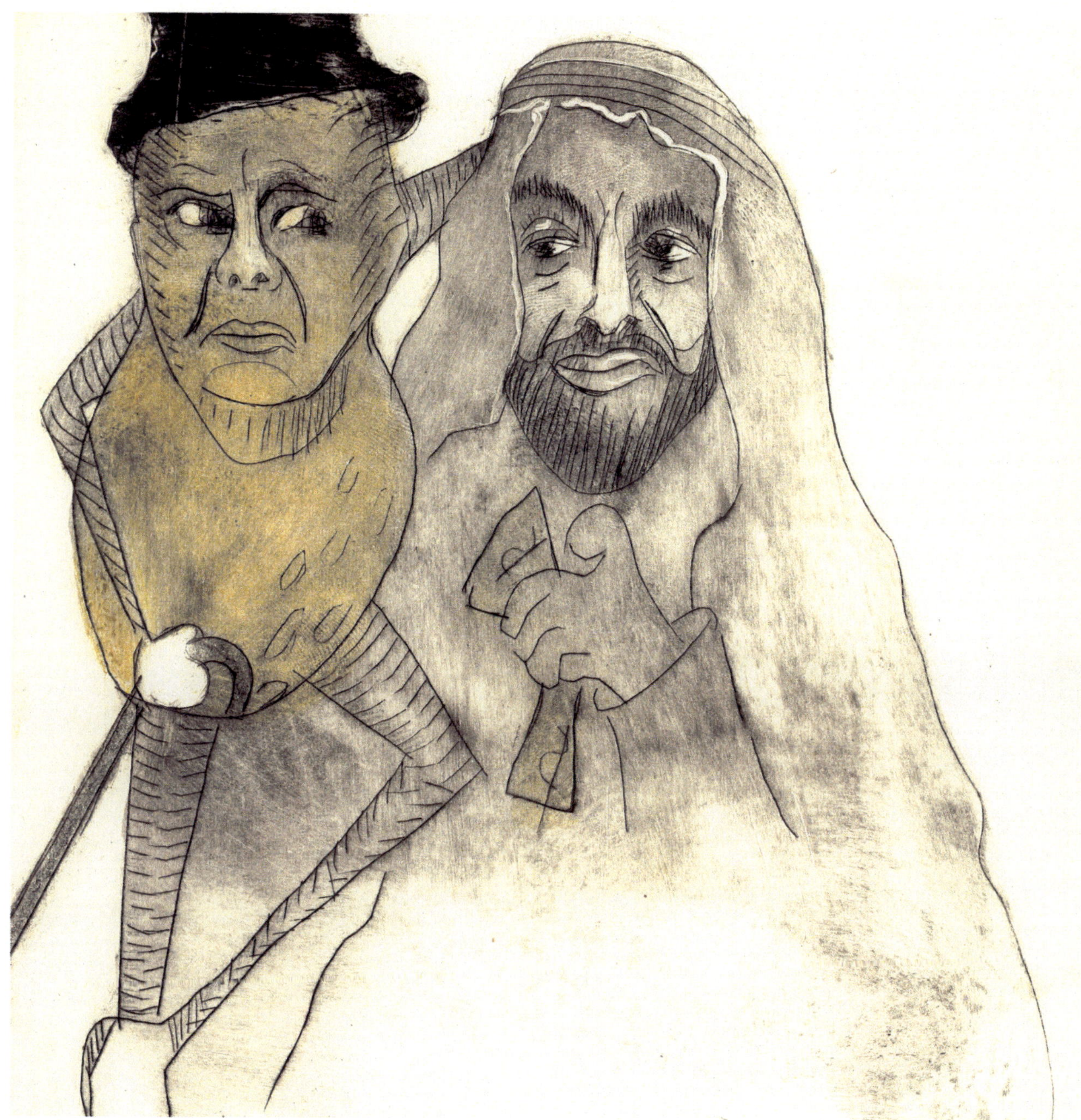

Two Faces

Portrait of Dr. Omeish: You would not recognize him from this portrait because in real life it does not LOOK like he has two faces.

He claims to be a moderate voice.

"Congratulations to those who have given up their lives … they are the spearheads of the effort to free Palestine."

> Dr. Esam Omeish, president of the Muslim American Society, "largest grassroots Muslim group in America", at a rally, October 6, 2000, in front of the Israeli Embassy to the United States, Washington DC.

"You have learned the way, that you have known that the jihad way is the way to liberate your land…Put an end to military aid to Israel. Conquer their state sponsored terrorism."

> Dr. Esam Omeish at a Jerusalem Day Rally, December 22, 2000 at Lafayette Park, Washington, DC.

Dr. Omesh, don't you know YouTube is watching?

dry point and monoprint
on paper printed
at sokolpress

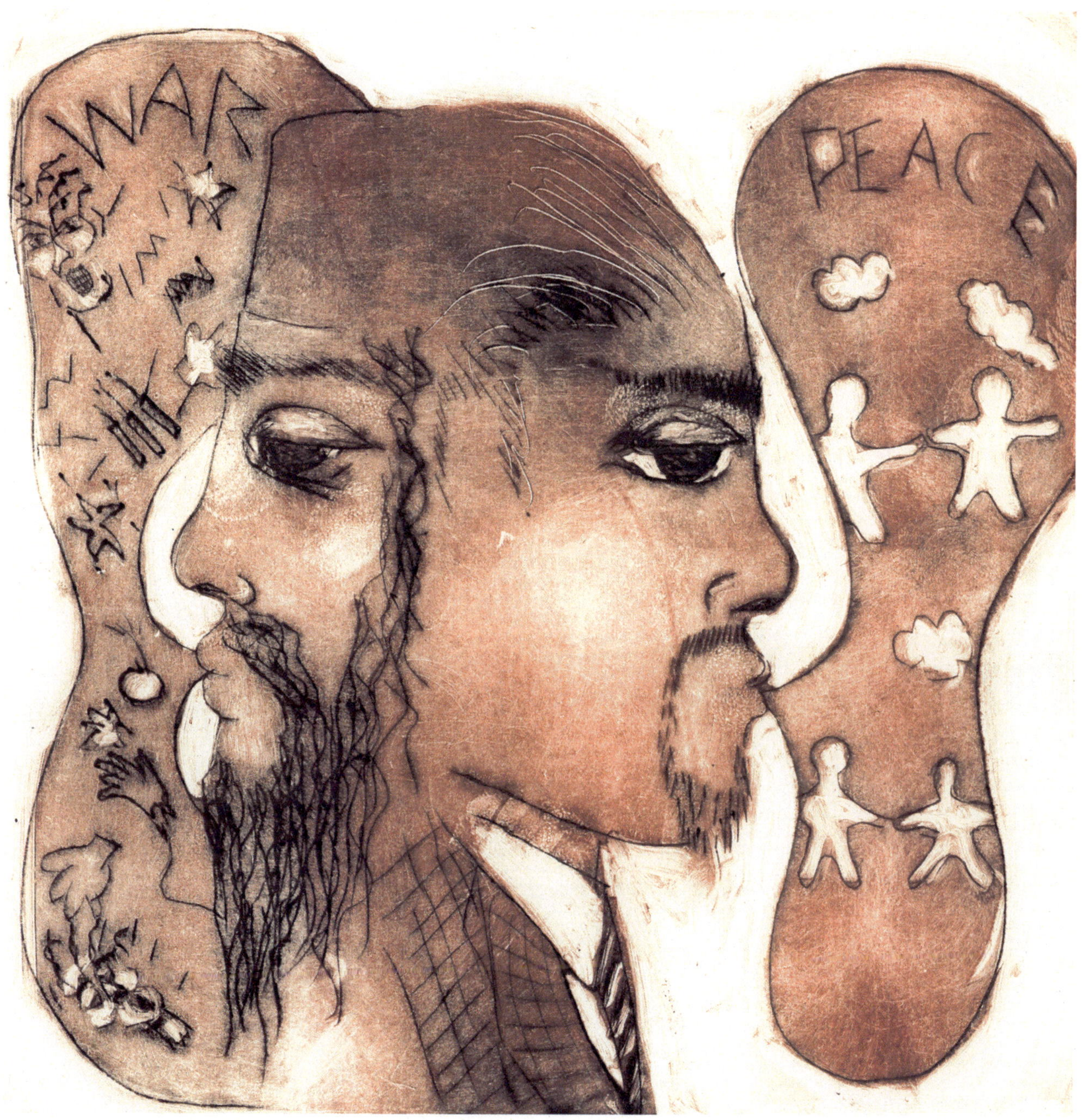

WAR
PEACE

The German Israeli Lobby

Today the contemporary German Israeli lobby meets at the cemetery.

reduction woodcut
on paper printed
at sokolpress

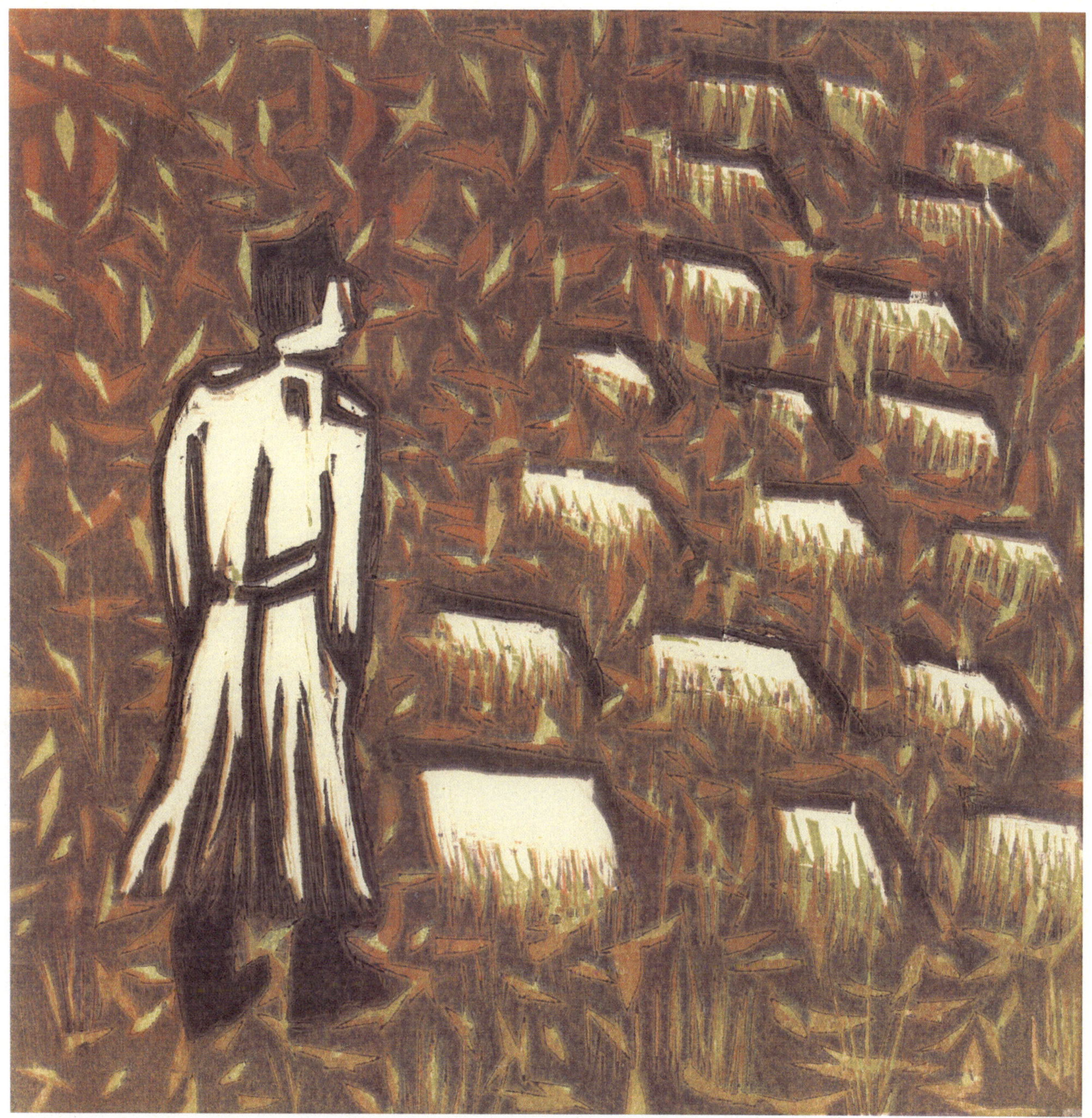

Peace Gandhi Style?

Do Jews have a suicidal capacity for compassion and dignity? Jews are
expected to sacrifice everything for peace including themselves. Mahatma
Gandhi advised the Jews in 1938 to offer their throats like lambs to the
Germans, so at least they would keep their dignity. Gandhi admonished the
Jews for violence, but ignored the violence of Arabs. It is obvious that Gandhi's
motivation was to use his anti-Jewish stand as a "peace" offering to the Muslim
world so he could bring peace between Muslims and Hindus. A balanced view
on Gandhi's part toward Israel would have set the Muslims further against the
Hindus. Jews became a pawn in his game. This of course was not the first time
or last time Jews were used as political scapegoats.

In 2008, Gandhi's fifth grandson, Arun Gandhi, co-founder of the M.K. Gandhi
Institute for Nonviolence at the University of Rochester, called the Jews the
largest players in a "cult of violence" which would destroy humanity. The world
is getting angry at the Jews, he said, for holding on to the Holocaust and
Jews should get over it. He obviously chooses not to take the violent faction of
Islam seriously. Criticizing peace icons is not popular, but it is not hard to
see that there would be no Jews on earth had Mahatma Gandhi had his
way. Did Gandhi not recognize his own Golem? His own rage and destructive
ability? You sometimes hear the statement that the Israeli settlements and
disputed territories in Israel create a moral backfire on Israel. Israel becomes
its own moral victim in a new dilemma of power... Well, yes, but what powerful
government is not in some moral dilemma that needs to be solved? The fact is
that as soon as any victim gets real power they have to face moral dilemmas.

An Israeli peace activist, Yonatan Shapira, was asked, "If we give up all
territories, we let Palestinian weapons close to our population centers. How can
we protect Jews in that event?"

His answer: "We cannot keep Israelis safe, but we must try this, no matter the
cost." This man has a grandiose or foolish image of how saintly Jews are. As
far as saintliness goes, a Jew is just like anyone else.

Here is another example of an irrational expectation of Jewish suicidality.

monoprint on paper
printed at sokolpress

50

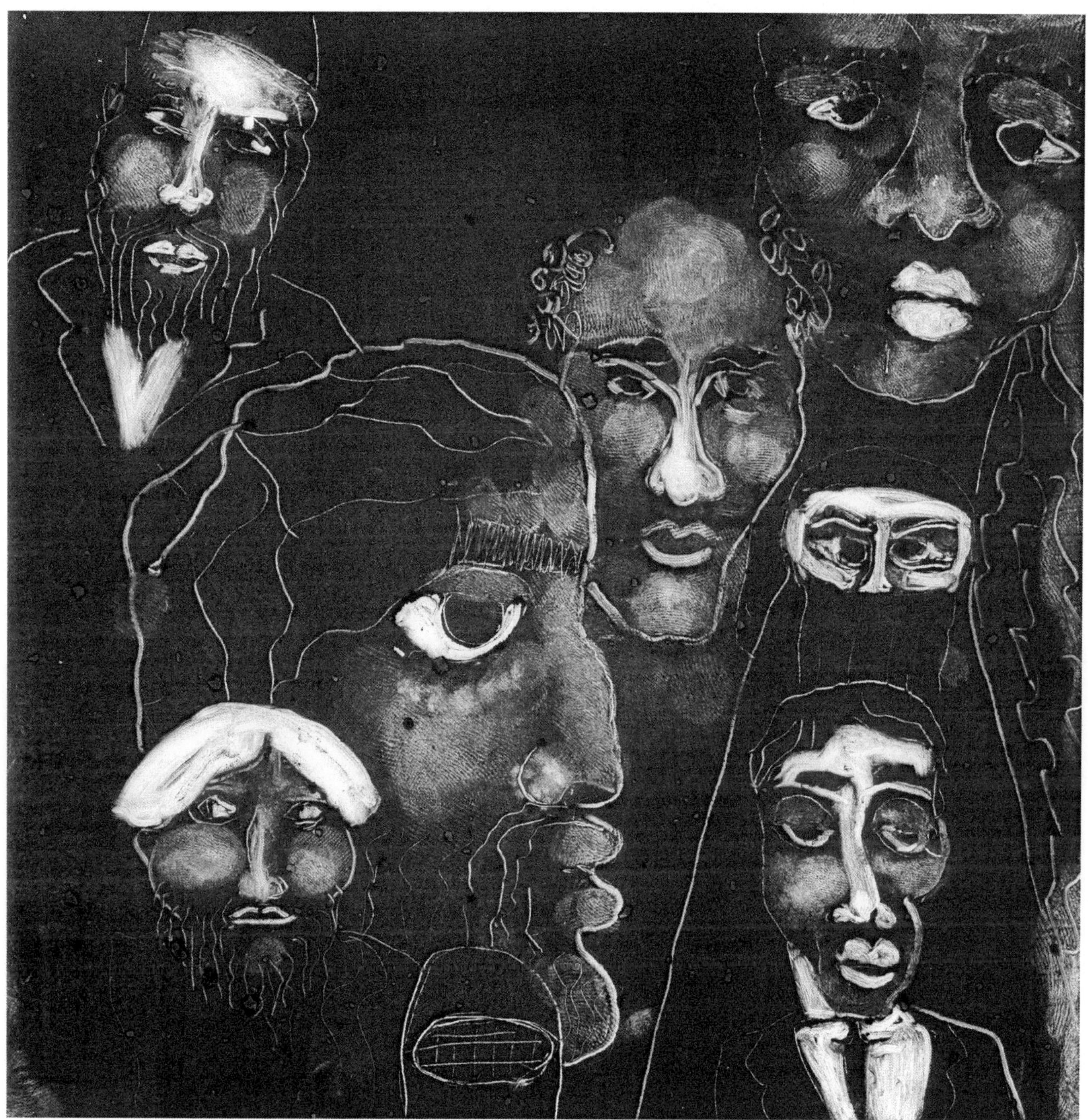

Friends

Friends, separated by politics.

Invisible emotions, allegiances, responsibilities…walls.

woodcut with chine collé
on paper printed
at sokolpress

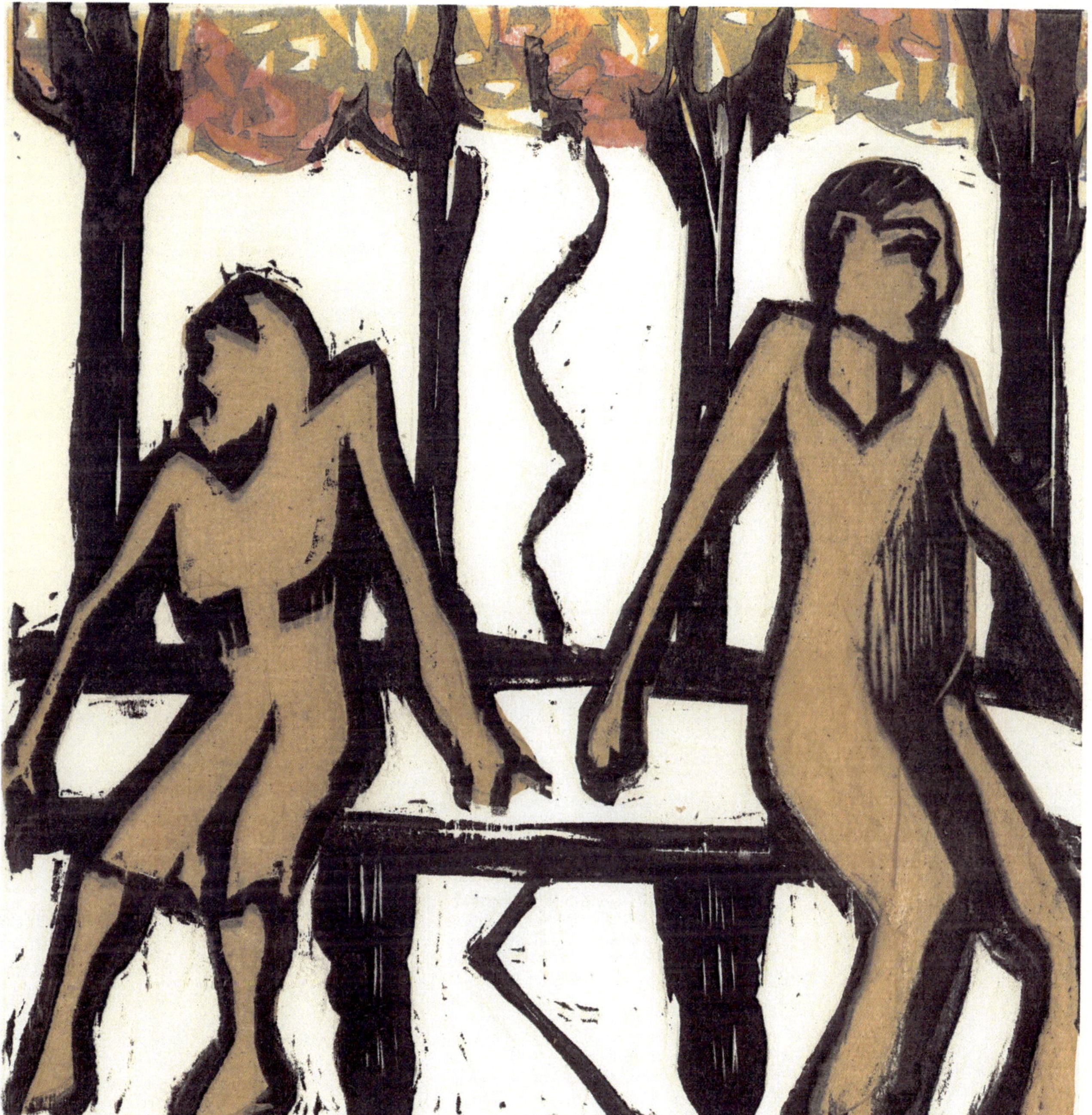

The Jewish Identity Office

I would like to trade in my Jewish I.D.

Sorry, office closed

collage and monoprint
on paper printed
at sokolpress

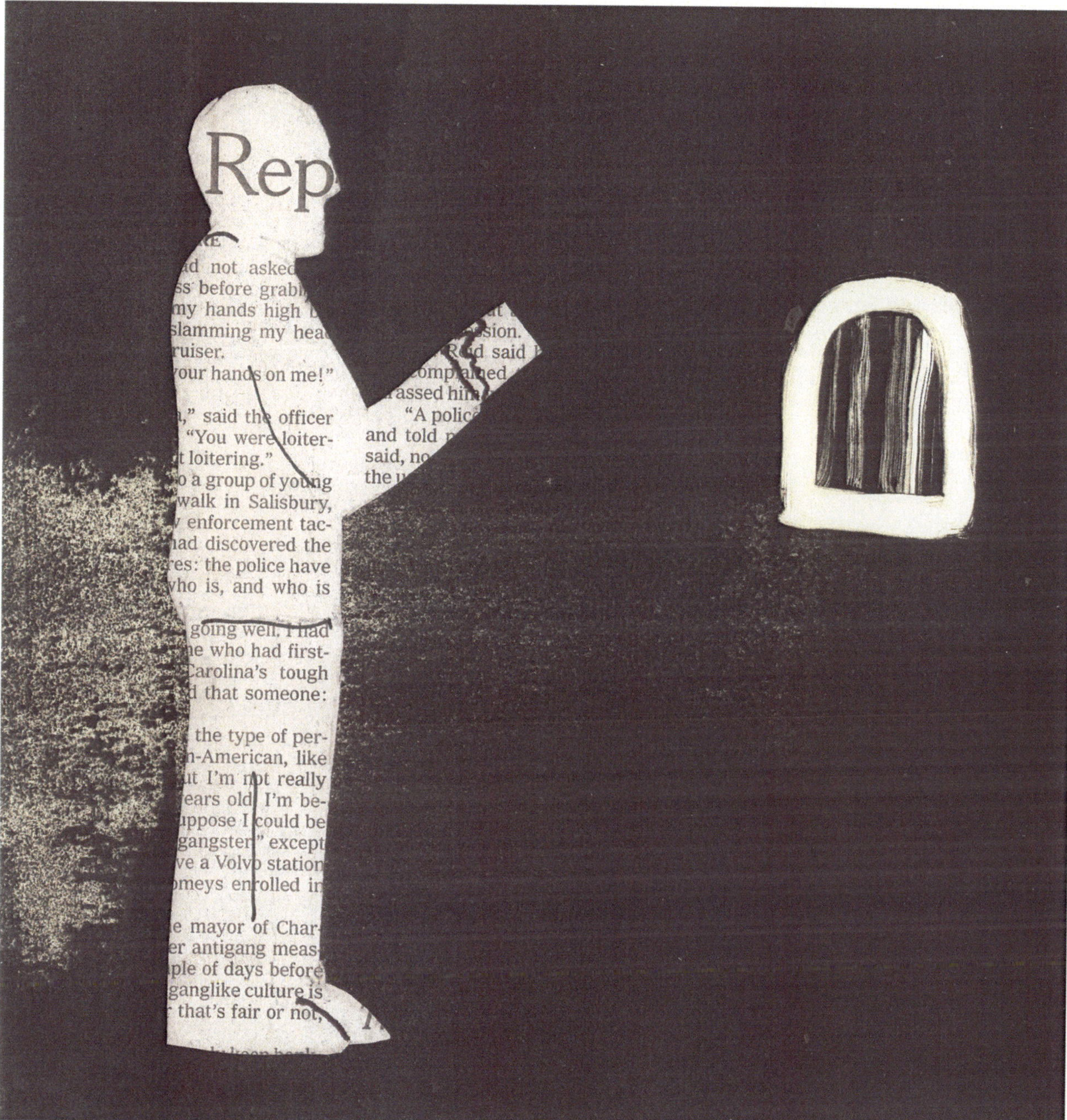

Rep
not asked
ss before grab
my hands high
slamming my hea
ruiser.
your hands on me!"
," said the officer
"You were loiter-
t loitering."
o a group of young
walk in Salisbury,
w enforcement tac-
had discovered the
res: the police have
who is, and who is
going well. I had
ne who had first-
Carolina's tough
d that someone:
the type of per-
n-American, like
ut I'm not really
ears old. I'm be-
uppose I could be
gangster" except
ve a Volvo station
meys enrolled in
e mayor of Char-
er antigang meas-
ple of days before
ganglike culture is
that's fair or not,
sion.
Rud said
complained
assed him
"A polic
and told
said, no
the u

The Golem: "Your eyes have seen my unformed substance"
(Psalm 139:16)

The Golem is a Monster

The Golem is a Savior

The Golem is the unformed self, the most insubstantial and most powerful
essence in you.

The Golem is the self buried in humanity. He comes forth in the most primitive
manner when survival is threatened. The Golem is the source of creative
solutions and destruction.

woodcut on paper
printed at sokolpress

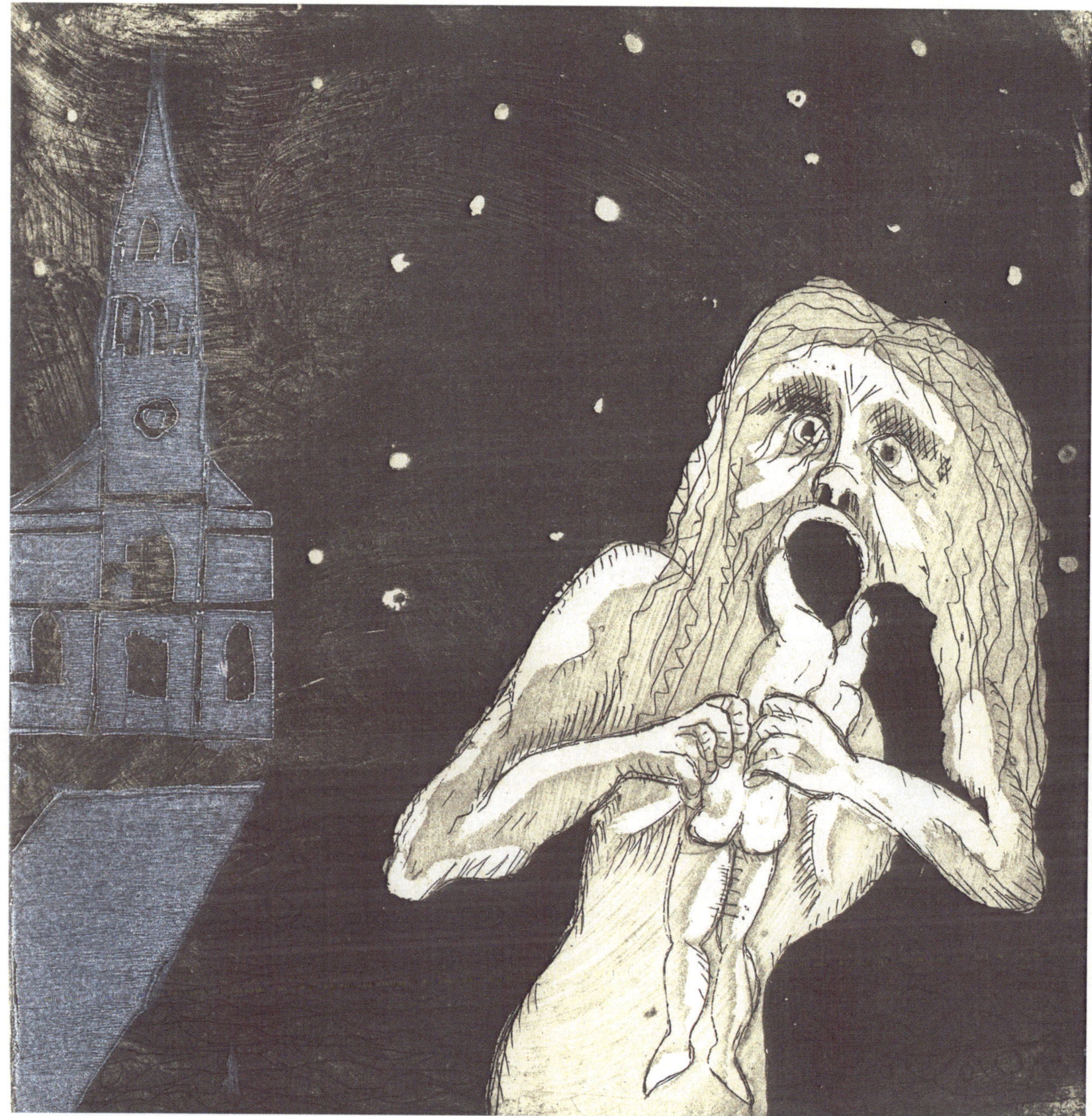

SOURCES & FURTHER READING

INTRODUCTION

Guhname, R. (2007, April 6). *Inductivist*. Retrieved May 12, 2008 from http://inductivist.blogspot.com/2007/04/mexican-immigrants-are-most-anti.html

General Social Survey. Retrieved May 12, 2008 from http://www.norc.org/GSS+Website

Loftus, J. (2004, October 4). The Muslim Brotherhood, Nazis, and Al-Qaeda. *The Jewish Community News*. Retrieved May 12, 2008 from http://www.frontpagemag.com/Articles/Read.aspx?GUID=0F956A35-69D8-4CC4-A05A-0F01651F14D9

Page 10

Wikipedia. (2008, May 22). Golem. Retrieved on May 22, 2008 from http://en.wikipedia.org/wiki/Golem

Page 12

Ye'or, B. (2006). The Status of non-Muslim minorities under Islamic rule. Retrieved May 12, 2008 from http://www.dhimmitude.org/

Wikipedia. (2008). Dhimmitude. Retrieved May 12, 2008 from http://en.wikipedia.org/wiki/Dhimmitude

Ye'or, B. (2002, October 10). Dhimmitude past and present: An Invented or real history? Paper presented as part of the C.V. Starr Foundation Lectureship at Brown University. Providence, RI. Retrieved on May 12, 2008 from http://www.dhimmitude.org/archive/by_lecture_10oct2002.htm

Kessler, G. (2007, November 29). Rice, Israeli official share perspectives; both women cite pariah treatment. *The Washington Post*, p. A16.

The Netherlands' view of the Annapolis talks. (2007, November 30). *The Washington Post*, p. A22.

Benhorin, Y. (2007, November 29). Livni berates Arab delegates for shunning her. *Free Republic*. Retrieved May 12, 2008 from http://www.freerepublic.com/focus/f-news/1932223/posts

Ben Eliezer, S. (2003, May 16). Jews from Arab lands to get money? The Week in review. *The Jewish Press Magazine*.

Belinfante, R. (2003). Resources for research on Jews from Arab countries. Proceedings of the 38th Annual Convention of the Association of Jewish Libraries. Retrieved on May 12, 2008 from http://www.jewishlibraries.org/ajlweb/publications/proceedings/proceedings2003/belinfante.pdf

Sullivan, A. (2007, August 30). In wonderful company [Jamie]. *Andrew Sullivan: The Daily Dish*. Retrieved on May 12, 2008 from http://andrewsullivan.theatlantic.com/the_daily_dish/2007/08/in-wonderful-co.html

Perelli, D. C. (2008, February 19). Blowing on the fire. *Reset DOC*. Retrieved on May 12, 2008 from http://www.resetdoc.org/EN/Blowing-fire.php

Page 20

Whisker, J. B. (1984). Karl Marx: Anti-Semite. *Journal of Historical Review*. (Vol. 5, No. 1), p. 69-76.

Marx, K. (1844). A commentary on Bruno Bauer's The Capacity of Today's Jews and Christians to Become Free. *Deutsch-Franzosiche Jahrbucher*. Retrieved on May 12, 2008 from http://pages.interlog.com/~girbe/Marx-Jews2.html

Page 22

Holmes, P. (2001). Brotherly enmity: No love lost between Afghanistan's "Last Two Jews". *International Survey of Jewish Monuments*. Retrieved on May 12, 2008 from http://www.isjm.org/news/article1.htm

Flexner, M. (2006, November 20). The last Jew in Kabul. *The New Statesman*. Retrieved on May 12, 2008 from http://www.newstatesman.com/200611200016

Aizenman, N.C. (2005, January 27). Afghan Jew becomes one and only. *The Washington Post*. Retrieved on May 12, 2008 from http://www.washingtonpost.com/wp-dyn/articles/A39702-2005Jan26.html

Page 26

Lipset, S. M. (1969, December). The Socialism of Fools: The Left, the Jews and Israel. *Encounter*, p. 24. Retrieved on May 12, 2008 from http://www.camera.org/index.asp?x_context=8&x_article=369

Bostom, A. G. (2004, September 22). Dr. King: Anti-Zionism is anti-semitism. *Hagshamá*. Retrieved on May 12, 2008 from http://www.hagshama.org.il/en/resources/view.asp?id=1823&subject=210

Page 30

Gordon, J. (2007, October 26). Hate at the altar-Sabeel in Boston! *Israpundit*. Retrieved on May 25, 2008 from http://www.israpundit.com/2007/?p=6263#more-6263

Anti-Defamation League. (2008, April 18). Sabeel Ecumentical Liberation Theology Center: An ADL backgrounder. Retrieved on May 25, 2008 from http://www.adl.org/main_Interfaith/sabeel_backgrounder.htm

Taylor, N. S. (2007, October 18) Starting the conversation. *The Jewish Advocate Online*. Retrieved on May 25, 2008 from http://www.thejewishadvocate.com/this_weeks_issue/opinions/?content_id=3832

McLaughlin & Associates. (2008). American Christian attitudes toward Israel and the epicenter. Presented at the Epicenter Conference, April 10, 2008, Jerusalem. Retrieved on May 25, 2008 from http://epicenter08.com/ISRAEL-natlsurvey-Christianvoters.pdf

Page 32

Wikipedia. (2008). Tomorrow's Pioneers. Retrieved on May 12, 2008 from http://en.wikipedia.org/wiki/Tomorrow's_Pioneers

Pipes, D. (2002, June 24). How central is Muslim anti-semitism? *Daniel Pipes*. Retrieved on May 12, 2008 from http://www.danielpipes.org/article/426

Wikipedia. (2008). Mohammed Amin al-Husayni. Retrieved on May 12, 2008 from http://en.wikipedia.org/wiki/Amin_al-Husayni

Page 34

Palestinian Media Watch. (2007, February 8). Hillary Clinton's full statement introducing PMW's report on Palestinian schools. Retrieved on May 15, 2008 from http://www.pmw.org.il/Bulletins_Feb2007.htm

Wikipedia. (2008). Tomorrow's Pioneers. Retrieved on May 12, 2008 from http://en.wikipedia.org/wiki/Tomorrow's_Pioneers

Page 38

Passner, D. (2006, July 26). Hassan Nasrallah: In his own words. Retrieved on May 15, 2008 from http://www.camera.org/index.asp?x_context=7&x_issue=11&x_article=1158

Lloyd, R. (2007, March). Golem on Church Street. *Peace and Justice News*. Burlington, VT, p. 5.

Goldberg, J. (2002, October 14 and 21). In the party of God. *The New Yorker*, p. 192.

Van Camp, J. (2006, September 23-24). Who is Hezbollah. *Counterpunch*. Retrieved on May 15, 2008 from http://www.counterpunch.org/vancamp09232006.html

Page 44

Dershowitz, A. M. (2007, April 30). The Real Jimmy Carter. *FrontPage Magazine*. Retrieved on May 15, 2008 from http://www.frontpagemagazine.com/Articles/Read.aspx?GUID=14F14A6C-2BBE-439E-929A-425288DA09E4

Ehrenfeld, R. (2001, November 29). Synopsis of Rachel Ehrenfeld's Evil Money (Harperbusiness, 1992). American Center for Democracy. Retrieved on May 15, 2008 from http://www.acdemocracy.org/article/invent_index.php?id=72

Aminoff, G. (2007, January 11). 14 Carter Center Board Members Resign. *Bear to the right*. Retrieved on May 15, 2008 from http://beartotheright.blogspot.com/2007/01/14-carter-center-board-members-resign.html

Page 45

YouTube. (2007, September 27). Esam Omeish in front of the Israeli embassy. Retrieved on May 22, 2008 from http://www.youtube.com/watch?v=sb8jKzrvT6l.

YouTube. (2007, September 27). Esam Omeish at Jerusalem Day Rally. Retrieved on May 22, 2008 from http://www.youtube.com/watch?v=Lajn3zOoWt4

Page 50

Ledeen, M. (2008, January 21). The Post, Newsweek, and the Jews. *Faster, Please*. Retrieved on May 22, 2008 from http://pajamasmedia.com/michaelledeen/2008/01/

Gandhi, A. (2008, January 7). Jewish identity can't depend on violence. *On Faith*. Retrieved on May 22, 2008 from http://newsweek.washingtonpost.com/onfaith/arun_gandhi/2008/01/jewish_identity_in_the_past.html

ACKNOWLEDGEMENTS

I would like to thank my printmaking mentors David Curcio, Hiroki Morinoue, Jeera Rattanangkoon for providing me with the opportunity to learn the expressive skills of printmaking. I would like to thank Carol Heffer, Terry Hauptman and Janet Beil for reading and encouraging the book project. Of course I thank Aaron Sokol and Janet Ballantyne for living with me during the process and adding valuable feedback. I also thank my publisher Ric Kadour and Kasini House for producing the book and exhibit. Others to thank-(thanking does not imply they agree with my points in the book)- Ray Rep for the suggestion of a wider audience, Marvin Fishmen for a first review, Francisco Goya, Honore Daumier.

ABOUT DAVID SOKOL

David Sokol is a printmaker from Burlington, Vermont. Born in Verona, New Jersey in 1947, David Sokol grew up in a suburban town of Jewish and Italian immigrants. In 1965, he went to Goddard College in Vermont and then to Sonoma State University in California where he joined the emerging field of Humanistic Psychology. Upon earning a Master's degree he returned to Vermont, where he practiced for over twenty-five years.

Having studied art at Goddard and working as a hobbyist throughout his life, Sokol took up art seriously in 1998 and has been working as a full-time artist since 2003. He studied printmaking with Hiroki Morinoue and Jeera Rattanangkoon at the Holualoa Foundation for Arts and Culture in Holualoa, Hawaii and David Curcio of Ningyo Editions in Watertown, Massachusetts.

In 2005, Sokol's work was included in "The Scrolls", a traveling exhibition curated by Mary Walker as a reaction to the war in Iraq. Also in 2005, Sokol's work was included in "Transitions" a portfolio of twelve prints by twelve artists from Burlington City Arts' Print Studio 250. This work was collected by the University of Vermont and the DeCordova Museum and Sculpture Park in Lincoln, Massachusetts, where it will be exhibited in August 2008. In 2006, Sokol was an artist-in-residence at Acadia National Park on Mount Desert Island, Maine.

Other exhibitions have included group shows at K Space Contemporary in Corpus Christi, Texas (2006); Firehouse Center for the Visual Arts in Burlington, Vermont (2007); and the East Hawaii Cultural Center in Hilo, Hawaii (2008).

David is a participant and supporter of the community printmaking movement and active with Burlington City Arts Print and Clay Studio in Burlington, Vermont, the Donkey Mill Art Center in Holualoa, Hawaii and Ningyo Editions in Watertown, Massachusetts. These centers are welcome resources for creativity.